God *is Not*
Looking for a
Part-Time Lover but a
COMMITTED PEOPLE

God is Not
Looking for a
Part-Time Lover but a
COMMITTED PEOPLE

It's Time to Stop Straddling the Fence

Belinda Nored

iUniverse LLC
Bloomington

**GOD IS NOT LOOKING FOR A PART-TIME
LOVER BUT A COMMITTED PEOPLE**
It's Time to Stop Straddling the Fence

*Scripture quotations marked KJV are from the Holy Bible, King James Version
(Authorized Version). First published in 1611. Quoted from the KJV Classic
Reference Bible, Copyright © 1983 by The Zondervan Corporation.*

iUniverse books may be ordered through booksellers or by contacting:

*iUniverse LLC
1663 Liberty Drive
Bloomington, IN 47403
www.iuniverse.com
1-800-Authors (1-800-288-4677)*

*ISBN: 978-1-4917-1014-2 (sc)
ISBN: 978-1-4917-1016-6 (hc)
ISBN: 978-1-4917-1015-9 (e)*

Library of Congress Control Number: 2014901178

Printed in the United States of America.

iUniverse rev. date: 01/23/2014

Contents

This Book Is Dedicated

To God the father, God the son, God the Holy Spirit, and to those who need spiritual direction, and for all to turn back to the unadulterated word of God, to motivate the believers as well as the non-believers to trust and have faith in the almighty God.

God Is Not Looking For a Part Time Lover, But a committed people.

God is looking for a people who will dedicate their life to serving him, and not follow after the things of the world. He's looking for people that will pick up their cross forsake all and follow him. 2CHORNICLES 7:14 If my people, which are called by my name, shall humble themselves, and pray, and seek my face, and turn from their wicked ways; then will I hear from heaven, and will forgive their sin, and will heal their land. NOTICE HE SAYS MY PEOPLE! A lot of time in reading this scripture we feel as though God is speaking to the worldly people, but he's not God is speaking to the body of Christ. We do not see the body of Christ as being wicked, but God is calling for the body of Christ to turn from their wicked ways. Everyone that calls himself a believer is not, we can accept Christ as our Lord and Savior, but there is a different between accepting him and having a relationship with him, and serving him. The Bible tells us that judgment will begin at home (the house of God). In order to make a turn Romans (12:2) says and be not conformed to this world: but be ye transformed by the renewing of your mind, that ye may prove what is that good, and acceptable, and perfect, will of God. To be a committed people for the Lord we have to have a changed mind set. The Bible tells us to let this mind be in you which was also in Christ Jesus. We must come from under the world way of thinking; he says to

1

be ye separated from the world. The Bible says we are in the world, but we're not of the world. God is giving us instructions on how his people can come together in cooperate prayer. Jeremiah informs us with his first letter to the exiles: Chapter (29:12-14): Then shall ye call upon me, and ye shall go and pray unto me, and I will hearken unto you. And ye shall seek me, and find me, when ye shall search for me with all your heart. And I will be found of you, saith the Lord:

A lot of believers have turned away from the things of God. We have not taken a stand as believers we have allowed the world to operate our lives more than God himself. People, we have become a perverse nation; God is making a plea for his people to turn back to him. We have disobeyed the commandments of God. The first commandment God has given is thou shall have no other gods before me. But we depend more on our worldly possessions than God. (2). Thou shalt not make unto thee any graven image. But there is an idol god standing on the water in New York City. (3). Thou shalt not take the name of the Lord thy God in vain; there are a lot of people that use his name in disloyalty with vain worshiping. (4) Remember the Sabbath day to keep it holy, but we find so many other things to do on this day that was set aside for God. (5). Honor thy father and thy mother: this means to respect our earthly parents just as we are to respect our heavenly Father at all time. (6). Thou shalt not kill. But we kill each other every day physically, emotionally, verbally, spiritually, and mentally. (7). Thou shalt not commit adultery. This means not to step outside of your marriage vows; not only between you and your spouse but also with God. (8). Thou salt not steal. Let whatever you possess be through proper means which is the right way. (9). Thou shalt not bear false witness against thy neighbor. This is a call to be trust worthy and truthful. (10). Thou shalt not covet thy neighbor's house; thou shalt not covet thy neighbor's wife, nor his manservant, nor his maidservant, nor his ox, nor his ass, nor anything that is thy neighbor's. NOTICE IT SAID NEIGHBOR'S. Your neighbor is any and every body.

We have allowed the order of God to be governed by non believers by allowing prayer to be taken out of our schools. We have put people in authority that do not acknowledge God. We have not taken a stand against abortion, nor against same sex marriage. These things are not pleasing to God. We have become the silent voice when God is looking for a commit people that will stand up and testify bearing to who he is. God is looking for someone that will say send me Lord I will go, but when God calls we turn a deaf ear. We say send me and then we allow fear of the world to overrule what we have commit to do for God. The Bible tells us that God didn't give us a spirit of fear but of power, love and a sound mind. We must realize that when God calls us he also equips us, God do not call you and leave you standing alone. All God need is a willing vessel that he can use to do his will. We must have faith in his word to know that we have power in us 1John (4:4) states ye are of God little children, and have overcome them, because greater is he that is in you then he that is in the world. Hosea (4:6): My people are destroyed for a lack of knowledge. Because thou hast rejected knowledge, I will also reject thee, that thou shalt be no priest to me: seeing thou hast forgotten the law of thy God, I will also forget thy children. In order to gain knowledge of God you must fear him. Proverbs (1:7) the fear of the Lord is the beginning of knowledge: but fools despise wisdom and instruction. Proverbs (1:5): A wise man will hear, and will increase learning; and a man of understanding shall attain unto wise counsels: but God says my people perish for a lack of knowledge. When you have no knowledge of God which is genuine wisdom then the world becomes your teacher (Satan). You begin to do things the worldly way by rejecting the ways of our heavenly father. The Bible tells us that the thief comes but for to kill, and to steal, and to destroy. If we are rejecting the ways of God, we have become a murderer, a liar, and a theft.

The Bible says that we cannot inherit the kingdom of God being carnal minded. We as believers must live a holy and righteous life and not as those that are living their lives as non believers. Jude (1:6-8): And the angels which kept not their first estate but left their own habitation, he hath reserved in everlasting chains under darkness unto judgment of the great day. Even as Sodom and Gomorrah, and the cities about them in like manner, giving themselves over to fornication, and going after strange flesh, are set forth for an example, suffering the vengeance of eternal fire. We the people of God have allowed ourselves to turn away from God just as the people of Sodom and Gomorrah, and the vengeance of God's wrath fell upon them. God is calling for an awaking of his people to see that we are serving other gods, which could be wealth, material passions, your spouses, your children. God says in his word put no one else before him. We have committed adultery which means we have left our first love. The Bible tells us to love the Lord with all our heart, when we love the Lord with all of our heart we want stray away. The world has become just as Sodom and Gomorrah, and we the people of God want turn and pray, because we are too busy fighting one another. We need to look up because our redeemer draws near. God is saying wake up thou that sleeps, arise and cry unto me and I will heal your land. God is now covering us with his grace and mercy given us the time to come back to him. Sodom and Gomorrah set as an example for God's judgment when we turn away from his will.

❧ *Keep you focus on doing the will of God.*

Jude (1:8): Reads, likewise also these filthy dreamers defile the flesh, despise dominion, and speak evil of dignities. But, as believers we must continue to grow in Godliness everyday of our life. There have been and always will be those who will attempt to divert God's people from their main purpose, which is to live for God. Whether angels or men, God knows how to deal with the rebellious, but believers are warned not to participate with any such persons. We must keep our focus on God at all times. The wicked appeals to the lust of the eye, lust of the flesh, and the inordinate pride. They will pretend to love God, appear to do good works, but as you watch them closely they are as the fig tree that Jesus cursed. They look good on the outside and good for nothing on the inside. The wise will be able to identify those whose object is to be god, rather than to serve God. It will take a deeply spiritual heart to know how to reach any who is deep into evil without being contaminated-hating the sin but still loving the sinner. We as believers must contend to our faith in God and accept no form of alteration. Reject anyone who teaches that grace is God's permission to sin. It's not and never will be. God turns away from sin. We must beware of those teachers behavior whose teaching includes such things as:

(1). Licentious behavior (lustful)
(2). Disrespect or rejection of authority
(3). Greed or the love of money
(4). Empty promises
(5). Straying from God true word
(6). Grumbling and complaining
(7). Motivation for self gain
(8). Speaking of them self and not God
(9). Building others up when it's to their advantage
(10). Campaigning or promoting himself

People of God we can not possess the full authority that has been given to us, because we continually alter the word of God to make it fix our need. Revelation (22:19): And if any man shall take away from the words of the book of prophecy, God shall take away his part out of the book of life, and out of the holy city, and from the things which are written in this book. When God say to love your enemy that's exactly what he means. He never said they had to like you, be kind to you, speak to you, smile at you or even acknowledge you. God's word is his word it stands all by its self. People in the world will hate you because that is a part of who they are. They have the nature of their father Satan, therefore we as children of God should not get mad with the things they say and do. Their mind is of a corrupted seed so they will act and speak what is planted in them to do. The Bible tells us that whatsoever you sow that shall you also reap. We are not to fall by the waist side or to be a slothful people in the word of God. We are to uphold to all the ordinances of Gods commands, and not to change it to make ourselves feel comfortable. As believers we cannot accept change and conformability if we keep revising Gods word.

The book of Matthew chapter 5 and 6 Jesus gives a list of commands on what to do and what not to do. These things are found directly in the word of God. Now, In order for the people of God to turn from our wicked ways, we must turn back to the unadulterated (pure or unmixed) word of God. Here's a list being taking from Matthew chapter 5 and 6: Matthew (5:23-24): Therefore if thou bring thy gift to the altar, and there rememberest that thy brother ought against thee: Leave there thy gift before the alter and go thy Way; first be reconciled to thy brother, and then come and offer thy gift (Forgiveness). In these scriptures Jesus set a law against retaliation, to discourage people from taking personal revenge.) Matthew (5:38-42): Ye have heard that it hath been said, an eye for an eye, and a tooth for a tooth: But I say unto you, that ye resist not evil: but whosoever shall smite thee on the right cheek, turn to him the other also (Do not evil because it was done to you). And if man will sue thee at the law and take away thy coat, let him have thy cloak also. And whosoever shall compel thee to go a mile, go with him twain. (42) Give to him that asketh thee, and from him that would borrow of thee turn not thou away. Matthew (43-48): Ye have heard that it hath been said; Thou shalt love thy neighbor, and hate thine enemy. But I say unto you, Love your enemies, bless them that curse you, do good to them that hate you, and pray for them which despitefully use you, and persecute you: That you may be the children of you father which is in heaven: for he maketh the sun to rise on the evil and the good, and sendeth rain on the just and the unjust. For if ye love them which love you, what reward have ye? Do not even the publicans the same? And if ye salute your brethren only, what do ye more than others? Do not even the publicans so? Be ye therefore perfect, even as your father which is in heaven is perfect.

Jesus is calling us as believers to be imitators of our heavenly father. Don't alter God's word its stands all by its self, and as the children of God we must be obedient to his will. God is not looking for a part time lover, but a committed people. He's not looking for someone that only wants to praise him on Sunday morning. God is not looking for someone that has to be encouraged by other to worship him. God is not looking for coward soldiers, that want take a stand for his word. God is looking for committed people that will Go into the entire world, and preach the gospel to every creature. The Bible tells us if we believe in the name of Jesus we can cast out the devils, speak with new tongues, and lay hand on the sick and they shall recover. CONCLUSION: If my people, which are called by my name, shall humble themselves, and pray, and seek my face, and turn from their wicked ways; then will I hear from heaven, and will forgive their sin, and will heal their land. Remember love conquers all things. Amen

"Serving the Lord will pay off"

Jesus stated in the Bible that as believers we will have power in his name if we have faith in him. (KJV) Mark 16: 17, 18,) These signs shall follow those who believe: In my name they will cast out demons; they will speak with new tongue; they will take up serpents; and if they drink anything deadly it will by no means hurt them, they will lay hands on the sick and they will recover. As believer's we are not to just follow Christ, but we must also believe. There are a lot of people in the church that's following Jesus, but for different reasons. Some people are following because they see others doing it; some follow because they are trying to tear down and to bring confusion to the body of Christ. The Bible tells us that Satan comes to steal, to kill and, to destroy, but Jesus came to give life and to give it more abundantly. Everyone is not following because they truly believe; some are following after what their (soul) mind is saying to them, not realizing we have to believe with our hearts. Our mind can be deceptive if it has not been transformed by the renewing of God's word. It's going to take more than your mind to believe that you can do these signs and wonders in the name of Jesus. God is not judging us on our minds; he's judging us on what's in our hearts. The Bible says the issues of life come from the heart. Be careful because your mind will have you thinking you believe, but it has to match up with your heart. The only way you truly know when it's in your heart is by getting in the word of

God. Romans (10:17): So than faith cometh by hearing, and hearing by the word of God.

We can't read the word of God once and think that it's in our hearts; we have to read God's word daily. The Bible says that we are to meditate on his word night and day. 2Timothy (2:15): Study to show thyself approved unto God, a workman that needed not to be ashamed, rightly dividing the word of truth. It's going to take more than just reading the word of God, faith shows action so not only do we need to have faith, but we need to walk in our faith. The Bible says that faith without works is dead. The only way to understand the word of God is accept Jesus as your Lord and savior, and ask God to fill you with his Holy Spirit. Once you have received Jesus and have accepted the Holy Spirit. Pray and ask the Holy Spirit to lead you to a church that's teaching the gospel of Jesus Christ. Than get into the word of God, allows the Holy Spirit to help you that's what he's here for. Spend time in fellowship with the Holy Spirit of God. Once you build a relationship with him, he will open the word of God to you to where you will receive the understanding and knowledge of God's word. The more time you spend in the word of God, the more you will get to know him and to have faith in his word. You will begin to understand that God's word does not return void. That's why it's important as believers that we are mindful of what we speak out of our mouths.

Mark (11: 22-24) First Jesus tells us to have faith in God. For verily I say unto you, that whosoever shall say unto this mountain, be thou removed, and be thou cast unto the sea; and shall not doubt in his heart, but, shall believe that those things which he saith shall come to pass; he shall have whatsoever he saith. Therefore I say unto you, what things soever ye desire, when ye pray, believe that ye receive them and ye shall have them. But in the midst of all that we must forgive. Don't go to God in prayer asking him for anything, if you have not forgiving someone in your heart; clear that up first than make your petition to the Lord. The Bible tells us that life and death is in the power of the tongue, so you can either speak life or death, blessing or cursing, it's your choice.

There is Power in the name of Jesus, but there's also power in the blood of Jesus. Be very careful with the words you speak they will either put you above or beneath. We have the power in God's word to speak healing or sickness and disease, to speak abundant or lack, to speak life or death, to speak victory or defeat. As children of God, when we go to God asking for anything, ask according to his word in the name of Jesus. Don't pray your problem, pray your deliverance, and thank him that you have received it. Walk in faith even if you don't see it right now, and thank him for it as if you have already received it that's shows that you trust God's word. God can do all things but fail, it's happening it's coming to pass just hold on and don't doubt God's word. Believe in God, believe in his word, believe in the name of Jesus, and believe in yourself. The devil will try and talk you out of your blessing; he will try and make you disbelieve God's word. Especially if you don't see anything manifest right away, 2Corinthians (10:3-5): For though we walk in the flesh, we do not war after the flesh. For the weapons of our warfare, are not carnal, but mighty through God to the pulling down of strong holds. Casting down imaginations, and every high thing that exalteth itself against the knowledge of God and bringing into captivity every thought to the obedience of Christ. He says the weapons of our warfare, are not fleshy, but they are spiritual. So, therefore you need to know what the word of God says for your life. You need to have it down in your heart, so when the devil comes up against you, you can stand on the word of God, and not be moved.

You can have the victory just as Jesus did when Satan tempted him. Jesus said what God's word said, it is written. God's word says in 2Corinthians (12:9): My grace is sufficient for thee for my strength is made perfect in weakness. That means anything you ask God for, his grace has already paid the price, it's more than enough to take care of all areas in your life. When you feel as though things are coming against you, remember Romans (8:28) All things work together for good to them that love God, to those who are called according to his purpose. So when you are walking in God's will all things are working for your good. Matthew (6:33) But seek ye first the kingdom of God, and his righteousness, and all these things shall be added unto you. So when you put God's word first, God's kingdom, God's mind set, he will not only give you what you need, he will open up the windows of heaven, and pour you out blessing that you want have room enough to receive them. (Ephesians (3:20) God will do exceeding abundantly above all you ask are think, according to the power that worketh in you. (1 John 4:4) Tells us that greater is he that is in you than that is in the world. So you need to know that if you have accepted Jesus, and have been filled with the Holy Spirit of God, you have power in you that is greater than the world. You just have to accept it for yourself and walk in faith. (Hebrew (11:1) Says Now faith is the substance of things hoped for the evidence of things not seen. So don't lose your hope, God's word is continually blessing, just stay in his will.

❧ *God changes us from glory to glory*

God is continually perfecting you, anytime you are going through trials in your life just stand on his word; he's bringing you into perfection. The Bible says he changes you from glory to glory, to confound our mind into the mind of Christ Jesus. The Bible says that you are the righteousness of God in Christ Jesus. God will soon have a church without spots or wrinkles. God is working off corruption, and bring you into incorruption, from mortal to immortality. Until then cast all your cares upon the Lord for he cares for you. Put on the whole amour of God, that ye maybe able to stand against all the tricks of the devil. Trust God he is well able to take care of you better than you can take care of yourself. God knows who you are, he sees your heart. Keep pressing toward the mark for the prize of the high calling of God in Christ Jesus. The Bible says let us therefore, as many as be perfect be thus minded and if in anything ye be otherwise minded, God shall reveal even this unto you. Therefore choose ye this day whom ye will serve, choose Jesus, there's an eternal reward, it will pay off just hold on a little while longer to God's unchanging hand. The Bible tells us that weeping may endure for a night, but joy comes in the morning, (tell yourself it's morning time.).

If we Christians will take care of the household of God, God will take care of us. For we are his workmanship, created in Christ Jesus unto good works, which God has before ordained that we should walk in them, form henceforth let no man trouble you: For you bear in your body the marks of the Lord Jesus. (John 3:16) says God gave us his only begotten son, that we are saved through him. The Bible says for by grace ye are saved through faith, and not of yourselves it is the gift of God. God did this because he loves us, his children, and he wants the best for us. Matthew (6: 25) Take no thought saying, what shall we eat? Or what shall we drink? Or where withal shall we be clothed? God knows what we need, and he has already made provision for us. We just have to seek him and his righteousness first. Don't tell Jesus I give my life to you, and you give him the keys and tell him that he is only premised in certain areas of your life. And the doors are locked to the other areas. Ask yourself a question is that fare? Jesus offers every part of himself and we only offer what we want him to have.

No you not that you were bought with a price, and that you are not your own, your body is the temple of the Holy Spirit of God. Go to God with everything in prayer and thanksgiving, and remember God is no respect of person. Love God with all of your heart, soul and might, and love other as Jesus loves you. Love covers a multitude of sin. Don't be like the Pharisees looking for glory from men, but glorify your heavenly Father in everything you do. Serve the Lord God with all your heart and lean not unto your own understanding and he shall direct your path. Serving the Lord will pay off, if you accept him into your heart today it will pay off right now. You can than look back over your life and say now unto him that is able to keep you from falling, and to present you faultless before the presence of his glory with exceeding joy, To the only wise God our Savior, be glory and majesty, dominion and power, both now and ever, Amen.

Building on Things Eternal

Only what we do for the kingdom of God will last, Jesus is our strong foundation in everything we do. Everything that we do here for the Lord is a way of storing up spiritual blessing in heaven for us. The book of Genesis Chapter 11 tells us that the people had a goal in mind; they wanted to build them a city and a tower whose top may reach heaven. They wanted to make a name for themselves. The people of Babel had the right ideal working together in unity, but they had the wrong motive and the wrong foundation. They were out to build them a name and more importantly they left out God. A lot of times we have great ideals but the wrong foundation. Jesus said in Matthew (7:24-27) Therefore whosoever heareth these saying of mine, and doeth them, I will liken him unto a wise man, which build his house upon a rock: And the rain descended, and the floods came, and the wind blew, and beat upon that house; and it fell not: for it was founded upon a rock. And everyone that heareth these sayings of mine, and doeth them not shall be likened unto a foolish man, which build his house upon the sand. And the rain descended, and the floods came, and the wind blew, and beat upon that house; and it fell: and great was the fall of it. As believer's anything we do should be centered on Jesus in order for it to stand. When we leave out the foundation nothing in our lives will last. The people of Babel shows us that there is strength in unity, that we can accomplish anything together,

Philippians (4:13) says that I can do all things through Christ which strengtheneth me.

1John (4:4) lets us know that we have a power in us that is greater than he that is in the world. We have to know that by faith we can do just what God says we can do. We must always build on that solid rock, which is Jesus, and we must believe that he is in us. We need to know that every situation in life we have the authority over in the name of Jesus. If we look back in the book of Genesis (1:26) reads: And God said, let us make man in our image, after our likeness: and let them have dominion over the fish of the sea, and over the fowls of the air, and over the cattle, and over all the earth, and over every creeping thing that creepeth upon the earth. God gave the first man Adam dominion over the earth, and he lost it to Satan, who is called the god of this world.

God raised up his son Jesus the second Adam who redeemed the authority which was given in the beginning of creation, and Jesus passed that authority down to us. Mark (16:15-18): And he said unto them, go ye into all the world and preach the gospel to every creature. He that believeth and is baptized shall be saved; but he that believeth not shall be damned. And these signs shall follow them that believe; in my name shall they cast out devils; they shall speak with new tongues. They shall take up serpents; and if they drink any deadly thing, it shall not hurt them, they shall lay hands on the sick; and they shall recover. Jesus said in (Matthew (15:1-4) I am the true vine, and my father is the husbandman. Every branch in me that beareth not fruit he taketh away: and every branch that beareth fruit, he purgeth it that it may bring forth more fruit. Sometimes there's going to be things and people in our lives that God is going to take away from us, so we can grow in the things of God; so that we can walk in his prefect will, therefore bringing more to the household of God and to ourselves.

❧ *God has made provision for his people.*

God know what's best for us if we are going to be effective in the body of Christ. In order for us to walk in the will of God, we have to allow God to purge us, (to clean) out all of the things that are not like him. The Bible says we are to be just as Jesus is in this world, the Bible also says that we are made righteous through Christ Jesus. Now ye are clean through the word which I have spoken unto you. God's word is what cleans us of the old nature, that's why we need to stay in the word of God daily. (2 Timothy (2:15) says study to shew thyself approved unto God, a workman that needeth not to be ashamed, rightly dividing the word of truth. Abide in me, and I in you, as the branch cannot bear fruit of itself, except it abide in the vine; no more can ye, except ye abide in me. Stop looking at what the world has, the things of the world are temporary, and the things that God gives are eternal. There is also eternal life with God, through our Lord and Savior Jesus Christ. The worlds system is set upon lies, killing, stealing, and stepping on other to get ahead, and giving just to receive. The word of God says that it is better to give than to receive, God will bless you in what you do. Luke (6:38): Give and it shall be given unto you; good measure, pressed down shaken together and running over, shall men give into your bosom. For with the same measure that ye mete withal it shall be measured to you again. God has given us provision in everything in this life, if we just seek him first. Matthew (6: 34) says take therefore no thought for the morrow; for the morrow shall take thought for the things of itself, sufficient unto the day is the evil thereof. Stop worrying about tomorrow if God has already provided for you today, why you would not trust him to take care of you tomorrow.

(Matthew (6:25) Says take no thought for your life, what ye shall eat, or what ye shall drink; nor yet for your body, what ye shall put on, is not the life more than meat, and the body more than raiment. If God takes care of the fowls of the air and the lilies of the field don't you think that someone that he has breath his life into is more important?

But we have to decide if eternality is what we want and we need to make a choice. (Matthew (6:24) says no man can serve two masters: for either you will hate the one, and love the other; or else he will hold to one and despise the other, ye cannot serve God and mammon. You cannot serve the Lord and the devil, the spirit, and the flesh you cannot mix faith and fear. You can't be heavenly minded and worldly minded, one is temporary and the other is eternal and God does not dwell in a house of confusion.

God says that you are either for me or against me, hot or cold if you are lukewarm he says he will spur you out of his mouth. In other words choose ye this day whom ye will serve, if you are going to serve the Lord, serve him with all your heart, and if your choice is Baal than do the same. The book of James says a double minded man is unstable in all his ways. As believer's we need to understand that God is a spirit and those that worship him must worship him in spirit and in truth. Go to God with a pure heart when you are seeking him. If you don't know how to appeal to God ask the Holy Spirit to show you how to worship God. The Holy Spirit is here to be a helper so we can walk up right. The Holy Spirit helps us to labor toward eternal life, and to help us to be an over comer of the things in this world. We are to press toward the mark for the prize of the higher call of God in Christ Jesus. Everything that the Bible speaks on is coming to pass God has already ordained the future of the world. The fight has already been won, now you must decide who side you are on and be steadfast, unmovable always abiding in the work of the Lord.

❧ *Don't get caught with your work undone.*

The Bible tells us that no man knows the day or the hour, when Jesus will return for his church. Therefore be watchful and pray, don't get caught with your work undone. Don't be like the five foolish virgins in the book of Matthew (25:1-13). Then shall the kingdom of heaven be likened unto ten virgins, which took their lamps, and went forth to meet the bridegroom. And five of them were wise, and five were foolish. They that were foolish took their lamps, and took no oil with them: But the wise took oil in their vessels with lamps. While the bridegroom tarried they all slumbered and slept. And at midnight there was a cry made, Behold, the bridegroom cometh; go ye out to meet him. Then all those virgins arose, and trimmed their lamps. And the foolish said unto the wise, give us of your oil; for our lamps are going out. But the wise answered, saying, not so; lest there be not enough for us and you: but go ye rather to them that sell, and buy for yourselves. And while they went to buy, the bridegroom came; and they that were ready went in with him to the marriage: and the door was shut. Afterward came also the other virgins, saying, Lord, Lord, open to us. But he answered and said; verily I say unto you, I know you not. Watch therefore, for ye know neither the day nor the hour wherein the son of man cometh. Be the one who is caught up in the clouds to meet our Lord and Savior Jesus Christ, who will give us the crown of glory, and that eternal peace and joy. The Bible says that he will wipe every tear from our eyes, and so shall we ever be with the Lord.

What we must understand we can't work nor buy our way in to heaven. Ephesians (2:8-10): For by grace are ye saved through faith, and that not of yourselves; it is the gift of God. Not of works; lest any man should boast. For we are his workmanship, created in Christ Jesus unto good works, which God hath before ordained that we should walk in them. Your works want save you; you can't get to the father accept through Jesus. You can do good works in the calling by which you were called, so therefore seek first the kingdom of God, and his righteousness. Seek first God and his will and accept Jesus as your Lord and Savior, invite the Holy Spirit of God into your heart. Study the word of God, fellowship with the Holy Spirit and ask him to give you revelation and understanding in the things of God. To reveal and help you to walk in the calling that God has ordained upon your life. Ask the Holy Spirit to enable you in your infirmities, and watch God move in your life. We must be like Peter and keep our eyes on Jesus, if we take our eyes off the Lord we will never trust him enough to get out of the boat and we will continue to doubt. It's an impossible walk by our self but with God all things are possible. Jesus said that he would not leave us comfortless, that he would go and prepare a place for us and that he would send us some help, which is the Holy Spirit of promise; the spirit of truth. Who will guide us, and enable us in our walk of faith until Jesus returns for his bride the church body.

If you can see the true revelation that Jesus suffered and he was sinless, that he took upon our sin, because of the love that he has for us. Why shouldn't we join in on the suffering also, the servant is not above the master? 2Timothy (3:12) Says yea, and all that will live godly in Christ Jesus shall suffer persecution, Paul also tell us in the verse (11) that he as well suffered persecution, afflictions, but out of them all the Lord delivered him. The Bible says that God did not give us a spirit of fear; but of power, of love and of a sound mind. 1Timothy (6:12) says fight the good fight of faith, lay hold on eternal life. No matter what you have to go through in this life, no matter how many trials and hardships comes your way, stand strong in the word of God.

The reward is not giving to the swift, but to the one that endures to the end. If you follow after righteousness, godliness, faith, love, patience, meekness, and keep your eyes on Jesus you can't go wrong. In order to get to something you have to be willing to go through something. God can't perfect us if we don't go through things in this life. God is burning off the worldly man and bringing forth the spiritual man. He's changing us from glory to glory so that one day soon we will be able to stand before him without the fear of spiritual death. In the book Exodus Moses ask God to show me your glory?

God told Moses no man can look upon me and live. The Bible tells us in Romans (12:2) And be not conformed to this world: but be ye transformed by the renewing of your mind, that ye may prove what is that good, and acceptable and perfect, will of God. We must stop thinking and acting as a carnal minded man and start thinking and acting like a spiritual minded man. The Lord says come from among them and be ye separated, be ye holy for I am holy, says the Lord. We are in the world but we not of the world, we are just visitors passing through. Exodus (33: 20-23) and he said, Thou cants not see my face: for there shall no man see me, and live. And the Lord said, Behold there is a place by me and Thou shalt stand upon a rock: And it shall come to pass, while my glory passeth by, I will put thee in a cleft of the rock, and will cover thee with my hand while I pass by. And I will take away mine hand and thou shall see my back parts: but my face shall not be seen. We have a loving and merciful father who loves us unconditionally, all he ask us to do is put him and his will first.

Everything that God ask of us is for the betterment of ourselves that is what a loving father does, he looks out for his children, and that what God does for us. God loves us so much that he gave us the best that he has, John (3:16) for God so loved the world, that he gave his only begotten son, that whosoever believeth in him shall not perish, but have everlasting life. God did not send his son to condemn the world, but that the world through him might be saved. Jesus loved us enough to take upon our sins, though he was sinless. John (15:13-14): Jesus says greater love hath no man than this that a man lay down his life for his friends. Ye are my friends, if ye do whatsoever I command you. Jesus said ye have not chosen me, but I have chosen you, and ordained you, that ye should go and bring forth fruit, and that your fruit should remain: that whatsoever ye shall ask of the father in my name, he may give it you. As believer's we have power and authority in the name of Jesus and in his shed blood. Jesus never left us in darkness; he let us know what to look for on this walk to eternity.

John (15:18-21) these things I command you, that you love one another. He's letting us know that there is strength in unity, so stay in love one toward another. Hardships are coming your way, but if you walk in the love of God one toward another the victory is ours. If ye were of the world, the world would love his own but because ye are not of the world' but I have chosen you out of the world, therefore the world hateth you. The spirit of darkness can see the spirit of God in you that's why the world hates you. They are in darkness as their father is in darkness and you are in the light as your father is in the light. So therefore walk in the light, for he is in the light. Remember the words that I said unto you, the servant is not greater than his Lord, if they have persecute me, they will also persecute you, if they have kept my saying, they will keep yours also. We should rejoice and be glad in our suffering, because we are sharing a part of what our Lord and Savior endured. The book of James says to count it all joy when you fall into diver's temptations.

❧ We have comfort in Jesus.

We complain about the little things we have to endure, not realizing what Jesus endured for us. A sinful people condemned to eternal damnation, but because of Jesus we have eternal glory. But all the thing will they do unto you for my name's sake, because they know not him that sent me.

Jesus brings us comfort in John (14:1-4): Let not your heart be troubled ye believe in God, believe also in me. In my father's house are many mansions: if it were not so, I would have told you, I go to prepare a place for you. And if I go and prepare a place for you, I will come again and receive you unto myself, that where I am, there ye maybe also. And whither I go ye know and the way ye know. Jesus was letting us know that he died for our sins, to give us eternal life. Now he's getting our house ready for us to come home to be with him in heaven. When the appointed time comes he will come back for his church. In his place he would send another comforter, which was the Holy Spirit. To help us to walk upright, to reveal all truth to us, to bring things back to our remembrance, to guide us on this spiritual walk. John (14:6) I am the way, the truth, and the life, no man cometh unto the father, but by me. Jesus is our way to heaven, there is no other way. Jesus is our truth concerning all things in heaven, in the earth, and under the earth. Jesus is our only way to eternal life, and as long as God is on our side we are more than the world can be against us. Romans (8:28) says all thing work together for the good to them that love God, and to those who are the called according to his purpose. So, hold on to God's unchanging hand and everything will be alright. 1 John (4:4) says greater is he that is in the Us than he that is in the world.

Isaiah (54:17) No weapon that is formed against thee shall proper and every tongue that shall rise up against thee in judgment thou shalt condemn. He says the weapon will form but it will not proper. If we just stand strong on the word of God and not waver in our belief in God's word, we will be victorious. If we are wavering that means we are unstable in trusting his word. A double minded man has not chosen who side he trust in. Isaiah (55:8, 9, 11) for my thoughts are not your thoughts, neither are your ways, saith the Lord. For as the heavens are higher than the earth, so are my ways higher than your ways, and my thoughts than your thoughts. So shall my words be that goeth forth out of my mouth, it shall not return unto me void, but it shall accomplish that which I please, and it shall prosper in the thing whereto I sent it. God has made provision for everything in this life and the next life for us. When you put your life in God's hands leave it there, God is well able, and his timing is perfect. Trust and believe in God, remember his word will not return void, let him be your guide to eternal life.

Satan Has No Power over Us

It is important as believers that we get our mind in line with Christ Jesus. Philippians (2:5) Let this mind be in you which was also in Christ Jesus. It's simply saying line our mind up with the thinking of Jesus. Our focus should be on the will of God, just as Jesus was. Jesus said in John (6:38) for I came down from heaven not to do my will, but the will of him that sent me. The only way to do that as believers, is to study the word of God, 2 Timothy (2:15) study to shew thyself approved unto God, a workman that needeth not to be ashamed, rightly dividing the word of truth. The only way we can imitate Christ is by learning who he is, what he did, what he said, and how he walked. We can't win the battle of our mind by walking in the flesh, because the flesh knows no good thing. The battle starts in the mind, in our imagination, our thoughts, and our dreams. 2Corinthians (10:5) castings down imaginations and every high thing that exalteth itself against the knowledge of God, and bringing into captivity every thought to the obedience of Christ. Every time a thought is presented to us that does not line up with the word of God we are to take authority over it in the name of Jesus. The Bible says that every good and perfect gift comes from above. God is not the author of evil thoughts, God is love and in him there is no darkness at all.

When a thought is presented to you, and you don't cast it down, you allow a seed to be planted in your spirit that will produce after its kind. Whatever you sow, you shall also reap weather good or bad. Galatians (6:7, 8): Be not deceived, God is not mocked: for whatsoever a man soweth, that shall he also reap. For he that soweth to his flesh shall of the flesh reap corruption; but he that soweth to the spirit shall of the spirit reap life everlasting. Mark (11:23) says for verily I say unto you, that whosoever shall say unto this mountain, be thou removed and be thou cast into the sea; and shall not doubt in his heart, but shall believe that those things which he saith shall come to pass; he shall have whatsoever he saith. You allow those thoughts to take root in your spirit by thinking on them continually, and speaking them out, you will soon give birth to what you have allowed to grow in your heart. The more you think on those thoughts the more they grow. Don't think because you have not thought about them for months or even a year, that they're gone, they're not. Don't let the devil deceive you into thinking that thoughts are harmless, that your thoughts are no big deal. Why do you think that so many people in the world are killing, stealing, and destroying one another? Those thoughts are of the wicked one Satan.

John (10:10): The thief cometh not, but for to steal, and to kill, and to destroy: I am come that they might have life, and that they might have it more abundantly. When Jesus took our sins and nails them to the cross, he also nailed all these evil thoughts with him. But for some reason we keep picking up everything that he buried when he died in our place. We need to stop giving place to the devil, the devil devices or thoughts, ideas, and suggestions. That's why you must let this mind be in you which was also in Christ Jesus. You must be transformed by the renewing of your mind; your mind set has to change from the sinful man, to the spiritual man, from corruption to incorruption. Romans (12:2) Do not be conformed to this world, but be ye transformed by the renewing of you mind, that you may prove what is that good, and acceptable, and Perfect, will of God. Stop thinking the world's way and start thinking the heavenly way. Put your mind on things above and not beneath.

Train your mind on the spoken word of God, by speaking and confessing God's word. In the book of Genesis, God created the world by his spoken words; there is power in the spoken word of God. Genesis (1:1-3): In the beginning God created the heaven and the earth. And the earth was without form, and void; and darkness was upon the face of the deep. And the spirit of God moved upon the face of the waters. And God said, let there be light: and there was light. (God said, he spoke) you are not deceiving yourself you are walking by faith and not by sight. Hebrews (11:1-3): Now, faith is the substance of things hoped for, the evidence of things not seen. For by it the elders obtained a good report. Through faith we understand that the worlds were framed by the word of God, so that things which are seen were not made of things which do appear. Hebrews (11:6): Without faith it is impossible to please him: for he that cometh to God must believe that he is, and that he is a rewarded of them that diligently seek him. Now you know that every thought that come your way, you have authority over them because of the spoken word of God mixed with your faith. You do not have to succumb to the thoughts that the enemy comes and bring to you.

You are no longer under the curse, but you are now under the blessing, through the shed blood of Jesus Christ, our Lord and Savior. Galatians (3:13, 14): Christ hath redeemed us from the curse of the law, being made a curse for us, for it is written, cursed is every one that hangeth on a tree. That the blessings of Abraham might come on the Gentiles through Jesus Christ; that we might receive the promise of the spirit through faith. You can live a sin free life, if you get your mind under subjection, and under the authority of the Holy Spirit of God. You want sin, because it is not of God, if you live in Jesus you also dead to sin. 1John (4:4) Says ye are of God, little children, and have overcome them: because greater is he that is in you, than he that is in the world. You have a changed mind set, a heavenly mind set. You have a choice don't become slothful in the will of God, and speaking his word over your life. Speak what God has already spoken in his word, he says that you can have whatever you say, if you believe. You can't keep your mind under subjection unless you pray without ceasing, die daily to your flesh, and stay in the word of God. Walking in the word of God, should not be something you do once a week, it should become a life style, a daily walk. When Satan the tempter comes, you have so much of God's word in you that you can say what Jesus said, it is written. We can't do anything unless we abide in Jesus.

The Lord wants you to have peace in your life, your mind and in your heart, John (14:27) peace I leave with you, my peace I give unto you: not as the world giveth, give I unto you. Let not your heart be trouble, neither let it be afraid. Now you are on your way to understanding that Satan has no power over a believer, his only devices are thoughts, ideas, and suggestions. The only way for him to have power is what you give him by acting on the thoughts that he presents to your mind. You have a choice to either cast it down or to entertain it the choice is yours to make, it only has the power that you give it. Satan cannot force you to do anything that you don't allow him to do. Don't do what Adam did when God gave him authority over the earth, he allowed Satan authority because of a thought that was planted by deceptive means. When there is a thought, ideal, or suggestion that is of a corrupt nature, you know to cast it down and bring it into subjection in the name of Jesus. Don't not allow a seed to be planted in your spirit, if so you will allow it to take root and eventually give birth to it. When you have control of your thoughts, you can than learn to control your emotions. When you learn to control your emotions, than will you be able to love unconditionally.

✎ *Learn to control your thoughts.*

You can walk in newness without envy, anger, strife, jealousy, hatred etc. it's all a part of the battle of your mind. God has already won the spiritual battle all you have to do is line up with what his word says. God will not stop you from doing what you choose to do, because he gave you free will and he want interfere with your choice. When you have control of your thoughts you can truly walk in the love of God, you can really mean it when you tell your brother and sister in Christ that you love them, without conviction. The freedom of learning to control your thoughts will result in truly being able to worship God. Bringing about a turnaround for the body of Christ to unit as one, to be on one accord. Once you stop giving your thoughts power by acting on them, than you will realize that you have giving the devil to much credit over the things in your life. You can have control of your thoughts if you learn how to follow the voice of the Holy Spirit. Allow him to lead you in all the ways of Jesus, and stop building Satan up to be bigger than what he really is. But you must be committed to Jesus. Satan can only produce a thought, an idea, or a suggestion and you have the power to say I rebuke you in the name of Jesus. Use the authority that has be giving to you, by the shed blood of Jesus.

Think about it this way God doesn't have evil thought about you, so why should you have them about yourself or anyone else. Jeremiah (29:11): For I know the thoughts that I think toward you, saith the Lord, thoughts of peace, and not of evil, to give you an expected end. God thoughts of you are of peace, any corrupt thoughts that come your way, or not of, or from God. God does not tempt you with evil or sinful thoughts Satan is the one that tempts you to do wrong. God may allow you to be tested, but he never tempts us. 1Corintians (14:33): God is not the author of confusion, but of peace, as in all the churches of the saints. God does things in order, and if your mind is confused with all kinds of sinful and evil thoughts, there will never be order in your home nor in the house of God. If there is no peace in your mind, there is no control in our life.

The word of God is our shield to protect us for everything that the enemy comes against us with. Ephesians (4:22-24): That ye put off concerning the former conversation the old man, which is corrupt according to the deceitful lust: And be renewed in the spirit of your mind: And that ye put on the new man, which after God is created in righteousness and true holiness. He says you must be renewed in the spirit of your mind, in order for you to have control of your thoughts. Galatians (5:16-17) this I say then, walk in the spirit, and ye shall not fulfill the lust of the flesh. For the flesh lusteth against the spirit, and the spirit against the flesh: and these are contrary the one to the other: so that you cannot do the things that you would. Take advantage of the Holy Spirit of God, he's here to help guide you through and enable you in this walk. Ask him to help you keep your mind on the things of God, to teach you to walk in the love of God. If you don't learn to cast down your thoughts, ideas, or suggestions that are not of God, your thoughts will soon become so strong until you feel like you have no choice but to act on them. That's when you have allowed your thoughts to grow so strong. (Example) Think about it this way when you act on your thoughts that are not of God you allow sin to manifest. Soon as the sin has been committed in you, then there come condemnation, feeling of guilt, and repentance. It's all a trick of the enemy, thoughts, ideas, and suggestions. Before you commit a sin that thought is on you real heavy, and after it's finished that thought goes away until the next time he presents one.

If Satan knows that you are easily persuaded he will quickly come again. God has given his word as our protection if you have faith in his word, God word only works in our life if we have faith in it. Ephesians (6:11-17): Put on the whole armor of God that you may be able to stand against the wiles (tricks) of the devil. For we wrestle not against flesh and blood, but against principalities, against powers, against the rulers of the darkness of this world, against spiritual wickedness in high places. Wherefore take unto you the whole armor of God that ye may be able to withstand in the evil day, and having done all, stand. Stand therefore, having your loins girt about with truth, and having on the breastplate of righteousness. And your feet shod with the preparation of the gospel of peace. Above all taking the shield of faith wherewith ye shall be able to quench all the fiery darts of the wicked. And taking the helmet of salvation, and the sword of the spirit, which is the word of God. You must line up with the word of God. God has giving provision for everything that the enemy can come up against you with. But you must speak the word of God, live by the word of God in all that you do. The word want manifest in your life if you don't mix it with faith.

You can't take authority over the enemy without the word of God. Once you understand how Satan operates, your mind is more open, because you now know that he can't force a believer to do anything against their will. All he can do is present a thought, idea, or suggestion. In Isaiah (14:12-17) It lets you know that Satan didn't control his own thoughts, when he was in heaven, that's why he fell from heaven, because he thought that he could dethrone God. It may have started out as a thought, Or an idea. That thought or idea started the first battle, which causes him to be cast from heaven. Satan may have realized that he felled, because he didn't maintain his thought life. (Now there's a thought, a weapon he could use) if he fell because he didn't maintain his thoughts, maybe others will too. You can maintain your thoughts by walking in the love of God, and meditate on his word day and night. Allow the Holy Spirit of God to lead you. Proverbs (3:5-6): Trust in the Lord with all thine heart; and lean not thine own understanding. In all thy ways acknowledge him, and he shall direct thy path. The Holy Spirit of God will tell you what to say, where to go, he will help you to maintain your thoughts life. It is imperative that you examine your thoughts, and if it does not line up with God's word, cast it down in the name of Jesus. By allowing the thoughts of Satan to take root in your spirit will eventually produce giving birth to sin. If you want to live a happy and stress free life, take control of your thoughts, equip yourself in the word and authority that has been giving to you. You can live a sin free life if you keep your mind on Jesus.

You are not under the curse of Satan anymore; you're under the blessing of the almighty God. Philippians (4-13) says I can do all things through Christ which strenghteneth me. With Jesus you are more than a conqueror. Philippians (4:4-9): Rejoice in the Lord always and again I say rejoice. Let your moderation be known unto all men, The Lord is at hand. Be careful for nothing; but in everything by prayer and supplication with thanksgiving let your request be made known unto God. And the peace of God, which passeth all understanding, shall keep your hearts and minds through Christ Jesus. Then he tells you what to think on to keep your minds and hearts clear. Finally, brethren whatsoever things are true, whatsoever things are honest, whatsoever things are just, whatsoever things are pure, whatsoever things are lovely, whatsoever things are of a good report: if there any virtue, and if there be any praise, think on these things.

✑ *Improper thoughts lead to sin.*

Those things which ye have both learned, and received, and heard, and seen in me do: and the God of peace shall be with you. You allow Satan to get the upper hand if you fell to maintain your thoughts, he is a deceiver. Satan experimented with this new found principle in the garden of Eden with Eve and it worked, here are some more examples of how he used people that didn't maintain their thought life, (Acts chapter 5) Ananias and his wife Sapphira, the book of (Luke chapt.6) Judas Iscariot, the disciple which was the traitor. Satan planted a thought, idea, or a suggestion, and for these people failing to maintain their thoughts, the end was destruction and will likewise be the destruction of the human race if we refuse to turn away from sin. Paul was speaking to the church for a reason. He was informing them that an improper thought life for a Christian will lead to sin. And that sin itself has an end, which is death. The Bible tells us that the wages of sin is death, but the gift of God is eternal life. In the book of Joshua it reads choose ye this day whom you will serve. Ask yourself a very important question; are you making heaven or hell your home? Satan living arrangements have already been made 666 Hell DR. Eternal Avenue one way in and no way out. We should be looking toward 777 Heaven Avenue. We need to realize that Satan is the deceiver of this world and the father of lies. Even Satan will have to give an account of his deeds. The book of Revelation (20: 1-3) says and I saw an angel come down from heaven, having the key of the bottomless pit and a great chain in his hand. And he laid hold on the dragon, that old serpent, which is the devil, and Satan, and bound him a thousand years. And cast him into the bottomless pit, and shut him up, and set a seal upon him, that he should deceive the nations no more, till the thousand years should be fulfilled. And after that he must be loosed a little season. Revelation (20-20:10): And the devil that deceived them was cast into the lake of fire and brimstone.

As a Christian, you know according to the word of God, (Hebrews (11:1) says Now, faith is the substance of things hoped for, the evidence of things not seen. It simply means that whatever you are believing God for it's right there, you just can't see it with your physical eyes; we need to have confidence in God's word. We must look deeper into what faith is, and the only way to do that is to study the word of God. By studying the word of God we learn what his word says and we also learn to trust him through his word. The spirit of God leads me to write this example. We are just like the apostle Thomas, we don't believe until we see it with our physical eyes, it doesn't become real to us until then. But the Lord says blessed are those that have not seen but yet believe. What the word of God is teaching us is that unless we are transformed by the renewing of our mind, we want be able to see the things of him until they are manifested in the physical realm. God is a Spirit and everything he does is first manifested in the spirit realm, so therefore we must take on the nature of God. We must learn our true identity.

Genesis (1:26, 27): And God said, let us make man in our image, after our likeness: So God created man in his own image, in the image of God created he him, male and female created he them. You will never understand what faith is, with a carnal mind set (fleshly) because the things of God are not for the carnal minded man; they are for the children of God. The things you can see in the physical world are being first manifested in the spirit realm, that's how the kingdom of God operates. By us not living in the spiritual realm we can't see physically those things we pray and ask God for. There are angels moving about bringing them to pass, according to his will. We must be like Jesus, have no doubt that when you pray to God, he hears your request.

And when you feel as though what you have prayed for has not yet manifested, remember God's timing is not our timing, his timing is perfected. Don't allow the devil to trick you into thinking that God didn't answer nor, heard your prayers. If you have committed your life to Jesus he says whatever you ask in my name the father will give it to you. If you have put God and his will first in your life, there isn't any reason God would withhold any good thing from his children whom he loves. The Bible tell us in 1Jonh (3:22) and whatsoever we ask, we receive of him, because we keep his commandments, and do those things that are pleasing in his sight. Our blessing can sometimes be delayed, but delayed doesn't mean denied. Your blessing could be delayed because of what is being spoken it's in the power of your tongue. God's word says you can have what you say, and the first thing Jesus tells us is to have faith in God. Mark (11:22-26) And Jesus answering saith unto them have faith in God. For verily I say unto you, that whosoever shall (say) unto this mountain, Be thou removed, and be thou cast into the sea and shall not doubt in his heart, but shall believe that those things which he (saith) shall come to pass; he shall have whatsoever he (saith.): Therefore I say unto you, what things soever ye desire, when ye pray believe that ye receive them and ye shall have them. And when ye stand praying, forgive, if ye ought against any: so your father also which is in heaven may forgive you your trespasses. But if you do not forgive, neither will your father who is in heaven forgive your trespasses. So if you are praying in faith and believing, and have no doubt in your heart that God hears and answers prayers you will be able to forgive others. If you have not forgiving someone clear that up and then make your prayer request to the Lord.

We are born into a physical world we are motivated by what we can see physically. That's why the word of God says to be renewed in the spirit of your mind, so that we can understand the things of God and to be able to trust in his word. But how can you have faith in someone you don't know? And without knowing God how can his word manifest in your life. The word of God says in Romans (12:2-3): And be not conformed to this world; but be ye transformed by the renewing of your mind, that ye may prove what is that good, and acceptable, and prefect, will of God. For I say, through the grace given unto me, to every man that is among you, not to think of himself more highly than he ought to think, but to think soberly, according as God hath dealt to every man the measure of faith. We all have a measure of faith that God has placed in every man since creation. So you must build upon that faith and the only way to do that is to get in

God's word. The more time you spend in his word, the more you will learn to love and to trust in him. When you trust in God than you have the faith to know he want let you down.

Isaiah (55:11) so shall my word be that Goethe forth out of my mouth: it shall not return unto me void, but it shall accomplish that which I please, and it shall prosper in the thing whereto I sent it. God is reaffirming us that his word will do whatever it is sent out to do. You can trust in Jesus. He said that he will never leave nor forsake you. Building a relationship with Jesus is just like anyone that you want to get too know, and that is by spending time with him. As a Christian you are to live by the word of God. The Bible tells us that we are in the world, but we not of the world, God says come from among them be ye separated. You must study the word of God daily so that it gets planted into your heart. Whatever you speak comes from the heart, weather good or bad. That's why you want to get God's word sown into your spirit, so that you can walk by faith and not by sight. 2 Corinthians (4:13): We having the same spirit of faith, according as it is written I believed, and therefore have I spoken; we also believe, and therefore speak. When you are of the same spirit with God you speak what you believe because his spirit worked in you.

✑ *Don't get weary in well doing.*

2 Corinthians (4:16) for which cause we faint not; but though our outward man perish, yet the inward man is renewed day by day. You must die daily to your fleshly body, the carnal man warred against the spiritual man, for the carnal man knows not the things of God. The Bible says walk in the spirit and ye shall not fulfill the lust of the flesh. The flesh desires the things of the world which are temporary, but the spirit seeks those things which are eternal, which are above and not beneath. 1Corinthians (2:9-14): But as it is written, Eyes hath not seen, nor ear heard, neither have entered into the heart of man, the things which God hath prepared for them that love him. But God hath revealed them unto us by his spirit, for the spirit searcheth all things, yea, the deep things of God. For what man knoweth the things of a man, save the spirit of man which is in him? Even so the things of God knoweth no man, but the spirit of God. Now we have received, not the spirit of the world, but the spirit which is of God; that we might know the things that are freely given to us of God. Which things also we speak, not in the words which mans wisdom teacheth; but which the Holy Ghost teacheth; comparing spiritual things with spiritual. But the natural man receiveth, not the things of the spirit of God; for they are foolishness unto him, neither can he know them, because they are spiritually discerned.

God gave us of his spirit so that we could understand the things that he has for his children. You want know unless you build upon your faith, the more time you spend in his word, the more your understanding will be open. When you study the word of God, you build up your spirit man. Whatever you feed gets stronger and whatever you starve gets weaker. So which do you choose to feed the Spirit or the flesh? God's word does just what he says it will do. If you pray and ask God for something, believe that you have received it, even if you cannot see it with your physical eyes it's there you just have a different way of looking now. Instead of looking with your natural eyes you learn to look and listen with your heart, your inner man, which is the spirit of God. When your mind is renewed it's easy to line up with what the word of God says without doubt. You can see it; it's just that you are now seeing with a spiritually renewed mind. When you start doubting and saying God didn't hear you, or I don't believe God will do it, or it's taking too long, you basically put handcuffs on God. That means you have cuffed your blessings. You have falling into doubt and unbelief. God can't work where there is no faith, just like Satan can't work in your life where there's no fear.

The Bible says that God didn't give you a spirit of fear but of power, love and a sound mind. We seem to have more faith in what we see verse what God's word says. That's why you must search the scripture daily, pray without ceasing, fellowship with the Holy Spirit of God, meditate on the word day and night, and in all you're getting, get an understanding. When you have doubt and unbelief in God's word, don't pray expecting anything from the Lord, because you have set a road block between you and heaven. You must trust and believe in God's word acting on faith. God has dispatched his angels to move on your behalf according to the faith you have in Christ Jesus. The angels are created to move according to the word of God only. They only respond when we pray according to God's will for our lives. If you really want to see God manifestation in your life, we should look at Paul and Silas as an example when they were lock in prison. They still knew that the God they served was well able to deliver them. Acts (16:25-26): And at midnight Paul and Silas prayed, and sang praises unto God: and the prisoners heard them.

Not only did they pray, but they sung praises to God, they wasn't looking at their surroundings they kept their mind on Jesus. A lot of times instead of keeping our mind on the author and finisher of our faith we start looking at our surroundings and focusing on our situation. We find ourselves lined up with the world instead of with our savior. (26): And suddenly there was a great earthquake, so that the foundation of the prison was shaken: and immediately all the doors were opened, and every one's bands were loosed. Not only did their prayer and praises to God deliver them, but, it also delivered those that were around them. A lot of times our prayers don't just affected our lives, but it can also bless others as well. When you have faith in God's word that means you have confidence in the testimony of Jesus that he gave of his father. The Bible says in Romans (1:17) for therein is the righteousness of God revealed from faith to faith: as it is written, the just shall live by faith. God operates by faith therefore we must live by faith in order to access the things of God. Jesus says in Matthew (21:22) and all things, whatsoever ye shall ask in prayer, believing, ye shall receive. He says if you are in prayer and you (believe) you shall receive them. So as long as you believe there is no reason God want answer your prayer. You are the only one that can hinder your prayers. God is not trying to keep any good things from his children. Why would a father that knows his children have a need hold anything back? God does not want us to suffer unnecessarily when he's able to supply our every need. Philippians (4:19) But my God shall supply all my need according to his riches and glory by Christ Jesus. So whatever your needs are God is able to do exceedingly abundantly above all that you could ask are think according to the power that worketh in you. There's a saying that says more faith, more power, little faith, little power, no faith, no power. There's a story found in the book of Luke the 8 chapter that tells the story about a woman that had an issue of blood for twelve long years. This woman was looking for help in all the wrong places. She was trying to find help in man, when everything she needed was in the Lord. She was calling on man, when she should have been calling on him that created man. Is this you? Have you ever needed help and looked more to man than to God? How many times did man, family and friends let you down?

The Bible tells us to put not our trust in man, for man will let you down. The book of Proverbs (3:5-6): Trust in the Lord with all thine heart; and lean not unto thine own understanding. In all thy ways acknowledge the Lord and he shall direct thy path. This woman heard about a man name Jesus passing her way. She heard that he was healing the sick and raising the dead. She had enough faith in him to know if she could touch the hem of his garment, she would be made whole. As Jesus passed her way she pushed her way through the crowed. When you can't see your way press on, when it seem as if you can't make it through, press on, when others let you down, press on, if the doctor gives you bad news, you keep on pressing on. She pressed on until she was able to touch the hem of Jesus garment, and immediately she was made whole. The Lord said to her woman thy faith has made you whole. You stop your crying today and pray without ceasing. Your weeping may endure for a night but joy comes in the morning. You must believe God is able to do all things, but fail. Your faith can heal you and set you free from all your situations, if you just trust in Jesus. Through Jesus we have the authority by faith to access anything in this life that we have need of that includes your healing, your joy, your peace, your finance etc. God, will open doors that no man can close, and close doors that no man can open. God has giving his children the keys to his kingdom. Matthew (16:19): And I will give unto thee the keys of the kingdom of heaven: and whatsoever thou shalt bind on earth shall be bound in heaven: and whatsoever thou shalt loose on earth shall be loosed in heaven. Amen.

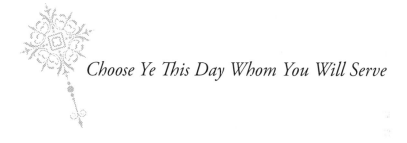

Choose Ye This Day Whom You Will Serve

We all have to make a choice in our life at one point are another, what or whom will you choose?

Joshua (24:15) And if it seem evil unto you to serve the Lord, choose you this day whom ye will serve; whether the gods which your fathers served that were on the other side of the flood, or the gods of the Amorites, in whose land ye dwell: but as for me and my house, we will serve the Lord. At some point in your life you will have to make a choice of who side you are on, whom you are going to serve. There is one God the father of all creation. The book of Genesis tells us that God created the heavens and the earth. Genesis (1:1): In the beginning God created the heaven and the earth. God also created every living thing that is in the earth. The Bible states that God created man in his own image. Genesis (1:26) And God said, Let us make man in our image, after our likeness. God created man and gave him dominion over every living thing that he had created. God is the creator of all, but that doesn't mean that every one of us belong to him. If you have not accepted Jesus as your personal Lord and savior, you must be adopted in to the family of God. The only way we can be adopted is through confessing our sins and inviting Jesus into our heart. Then believe by faith that the blood of Jesus has washed all your sins away.

If you have not giving him Lordship of your life then you still belong to the prince of this world, which is the devil.

John (14:30): Hereafter I will not talk much with you: for the prince of this world cometh, and hath nothing in me. Jesus was letting us know that Satan is the prince of this world. Light has nothing to do with darkness, for the darkness can't comprehend the light. Righteousness has nothing to do with evil, and faith has nothing to do with fear they are contrary one to the other. There are only two people that you can serve in this life. You are either on the Lord's side or on the side of the devil. Matthew (6:24) No man can serve two masters: for either he will hate the one and love the other; or else he will hold to the one, and despise the other. Ye cannot serve God and mammon. Joshua (24:19) Says and Joshua said to the people, ye cannot serve the Lord: for he is a holy God; he is a jealous God.

God is not going to let you put anyone before him there is no way people of God that you can mix good and evil together. The Lord says if you are not for me you are against me, there is no in between when it come to serving the Lord. When God gave to us he gave his best, and his only. John (3:16) For God so loved the world, that he gave his only begotten son; that whosoever believeth in him shall not perish, but have everlasting life. Jesus said if you are going to follow me, you must forsake all, pick up your cross and follow him. That means you must be willing to put everything and everybody behind Jesus; and you must also deny you self. God shared his son with us to save us, to give us eternal life. We belong to Jesus he paid our price, if he can give his life for us, then our decision should be to serve him. Ask yourself these questions, Did Satan die in your place? Did he shed his blood for you? Did he rise from the dead for you? Did he give you the same authority and power that was given to him by his father? Did he send someone to help you on this spiritual walk? Does he protect you, teach you all truth about him, or comfort you until he finish preparing this special place that he has for you? Did he tell you that he would come back for you? If you answered no to these questions, why is it so hard for you to make the right choice? What you have to decide is do you seek to be in eternal rest or eternal damnation, you can't choose both, and there's no middle wall.

No one knows the day or the hour when Jesus will return for his church. Don't get caught with your work undone. In other word don't get caught with not having made your decision on who you will serve. Tomorrow is not promise to anyone. You need to let go of everything that is holding you back from making a sound choice for your life. James (1:8): A double minded man is unstable in all his ways. James is letting us know that a person that has not made up his mind is drawn in two opposite directions. Your allegiance has to be made for either God or Satan, heaven or hell, the world or the kingdom. You can't serve two masters at the same time, because they are both the total opposite of each other. God is a God of love and mercy, Satan comes to steal, kill, and destroy. John (10:7-14): Verily, verily, I say unto you, I am the door of the sheep. All that ever came before me are thieves and robbers: but the sheep did not hear them. Jesus was letting us know that every one that came before him was a counterfeit. Therefore the only way to get to your heavenly father is by accepting Jesus as your Lord and Savior. I am the door: by me if any man enters in, he shall be saved, and shall go in and out and find pasture.

If we enter in through Jesus we have that assurance that we will be saved. Not only that but we also know that Jesus will provide our every need. We can walk around freely have peace which surpasses all understanding, and not have to worry about the cares of this life. The thief cometh not, but for to steal, and to kill, and to destroy: I am come that they might have life, and that they might have it more abundantly. The prince of this world existence is only temporary, but Jesus is eternal. Everything that Satan presents is counterfeit; he will make it look good with the natural eye, but will never show you what's behind the scene. Example: Have you ever seen something that was gold plated? Its looks good on the outside, but after you wear it for a period of time, it begins to fade and show its true colors. This is the way Satan camouflages himself. The Bible says that Satan transforms himself into an angel of light. But if you trust in God he can take off the covering of Satan. Sinful things are always done under cover, but God will do the exposing.

God says whatever is done in the dark he will bring to the light to show you what's behind the scene. I am the good shepherd: the good shepherd giveth his life for the sheep. Jesus says that if you love and want to take care of someone you should be willing to give your life for them. Just like any loving parent would do that loves their child. But he that is a hireling, and not the shepherd, whose own the sheep are not, seethe the wolf coming, and leaved the sheep, and fleeth: and the wolf catcheth them and scattered the sheep. He let us know that the hireling is someone that is getting paid to watch over the sheep's. The hireling does not care about the sheep's his just doing a job. And in the face of danger he will leave you standing all by yourself. Satan is just like a roaring lion he doesn't care about you he's a deceived, he will trick you in to thinking that he cares. Satan will give you everything you want to trap you until it's time to collect, a debt that is due. Satan only purpose is to get you on his side so that he can alternately destroy you. While Jesus on the other hand want to love and protect you by any means necessary. Jesus said that he will never leave you nor forsake you, that he will be with you to the end of the world. You have to make a choice for yourself. Choose ye this day whom you will serve. The Lord says that a friend of the world is the enemy of God. The hireling fleeth, because he is an hireling, and careth not for the sheep. I am the good shepherd, and know my sheep and I am known of mine.

✍ *God knows everything about you.*

Jesus says that he has a personal relationship with whom he loves and cares for so much that he knows them by name and they know him also because he spends time with them. God loves you so much he knows the number of hairs on your head. Matthew (10:30) But the very hairs of your head are numbered. God knows intimate things about you, because not only did he create you he loves you. Satan knows things about you too, but only things that you allow him to know Satan doesn't know how to love therefore he tries to counterfeit everything that Jesus does. If you open up your heart and make Jesus your choice you will know the different between real love and counterfeit love. 1John chapter (4:18) Says there is no fear in love; but perfect love casteth out fear: because fear hath torment, He that feareth is not made perfect in love. God wants you to have that perfect love that he himself is. God doesn't want us to live in fear, but Satan does because where there is fear it work against your faith. And when there is fear it gives the devil the right to invade your life. God want to give you prefect love so you want be in torment. When you walk in that perfect love of God, Satan has no right to invade your life, because perfect love cast out fear.

If you haven't made Jesus your choice who side are you on. Choose you this day whom you will serve, and remember tomorrow is not promise to anyone. The Bible tells us to watch and pray. We all at some point in our lives have to make a choice. God made a choice when he gave us he only begotten son (John 3:16). Jesus made a choice, the Bible tells us in John chapter (15:13-16): Greater love hath no man than this that a man lay down his life for his friends. Ye are my friends, if ye do whatsoever I command you. Henceforth I call you not servants, for the servants knoweth not what his Lord Doeth: but I have called you friends; for all things that I have heard of my father I have made known unto you. Ye have not chosen me, but I have chosen you, and ordained you, that ye should go bring forth fruit, and that your fruit should remain that whatsoever ye shall ask of the father in my name, he may give it you.

There are advantages to making Jesus your choice. He is the only one that loves us enough to take upon sins that were not his, but ours. He gave us his peace, John (16:33) says these things I about things that we will have to face in this life. He says in the world ye shall have tribulation: but be of good cheer, I have overcome the world. Jesus did something for us that we couldn't do for ourselves, and that was to overcome the world. Jesus brought us back into fellowship with God our father. Satan is not trying to bring us back in to fellowship with God he wants to tear us away from him so that he can destroy us. Satan has lost what he had, and he knows his fate is already sealed. Now it's about taking as many souls to Hell with him. People we are in a spiritual battle that is not our, it belongs to the Lord. There are so many people in the world today that think it's all about money, cars, big houses, clothes, jumping in and out of bed with different people. Others are married and turning to others instead of their spouses. Killing one another, stealing and breaking in people houses, for some reason people think it's easier to steal for what they want verses working for what they want. The Bible says a man that does not work does not eat. People are molesting children, raping women and men, same sex marriages. We hate one another because of skin color. There are those practicing witch craft, lying to one other for no reason. There is jealousy, backbiting, telling everything to others that someone has told them in confidence. These are the things of the prince of the world of this world which is Satan.

Jesus teaches us to love one another as he has loved us. Jesus tells us to forgive one another, to strengthen your brother when he has falling down and not to judge him. Jesus says to give to those that are in need, and to take care of those that are sick. To lead those to him that doesn't know the way. To take care of the widow who are all alone. Jesus said to visit those that are locked up, and to feed those that are hungry. To give water to those that are thirsty, these are the ways of the kingdom. It doesn't matter how much money you have, how many houses you can buy, how many cars you can collect or drive, how many clothes you can buy, these things are only temporary. Nothing in this world will ever fulfill you the way Jesus can. When God created man he breathed into his nostril the breath of life; and man became a living soul. That's why nothing or any one will ever give you that completeness and fulfillment, other than Jesus. Choose ye this day whom you will serve.

1Peter (5:8) says be sober, be vigilant; because your adversary the devil, as a roaring lion, walketh about, seeking whom he may devour. The devil main goal in life is to find someone to destroy. He's not looking to love you, him walking about looking to kill, to steal, and to destroy you. But verse (5:7) says casting all your care upon him; for he careth for you. Everything that the kingdom of God offers is everlasting and eternal. The kingdom offers a way out of no way. Accepting Jesus is that way out of no way, he's that hope when all hope is gone. Romans (8:28) says and we know that all things work together for good to them that love God, to them who are the called according to his purpose. In Jesus all things are working together for our good. We may not understand why some things happen, but we know if we belong to Jesus we can trust at the end of the day, he is working everything out for us.

It might not look like it, because you are going through so many trials and tribulations, but in Jesus you go through them you don't stay in them. God says he would not put anything on you that you are not able to bear. When temptation comes God has already made a way of escape. A lot of people in the world today think that because you are serving the Lord that bad thing shouldn't happen to you. But that's where we get it wrong, because the Bible teaches us that God rains on the just and the unjust. Matthew (6:45) Says that ye may be the children of your father which is in heaven: for he maketh his sun to rise on the evil and on the good, and sendeth rain on the just and the unjust. God is no respect of person, but if you trust in him, and put him first the Bible says that he will order the steps of a righteous man.

If you decide to turn from the world and make Jesus your choice, it will seem like all hell is coming against you.

The reason things seem as though they are getting worst in your life is because Satan had a hold on you, and now he's angry because you have made the decision to follow Jesus. And the enemy doesn't like losing anyone, as long as you are doing things his way life doesn't seem all that bad. So many people in the world are doing the same things until it seem natural. People have been sinning since the beginning of the fall of Adam. We have been doing wrong for so long until we believe that it's right, because that's how the prince of this world operates. When you accept Jesus as your Lord and Savior he transforms you out of the darkness of Satan, and into his marvel light. Than you can see clearly right from wrong, the good from the evil. You can see and feel the love of Jesus in your heart. Satan has blinded us to the truth; Jesus takes off your blinders.

✎ *Don't fall for the lies of the enemy.*

The Bible says that Satan is the father of lies. John (8:44): Ye are of your father the devil, and the lust of your father ye will do. He was a murderer from the beginning, and abode not in the truth, because there is no truth in him. When he speaketh a lie, he speaketh of his own: for he is a liar, and the father of it. If you haven't made Jesus as your choice then you are of your father the devil, and those signs shall follow you. But in Jesus these signs shall follows those that believe. Mark (16:16-18) He that believeth and is baptized shall be saved; but he that believeth not shall be damned. And these signs shall follow them that believe; in my name shall they cast out devils; they shall speak with new tongues. They shall take up serpents; and if they drink any deadly thing, it shall not hurt them; they shall lay hands on the sick, and they shall recover. Choose ye this day whom you will serve. Satan just wants to seduce you with the things of this world, but the things of this world are temporary. God wants to love and take care of you, and give you things that are eternal. Everything that the world offers, God offers also, but with God there is a promise of life everlasting.

Numbers (23:19, 20) God is not a man that he should lie; neither the son of man that he should repent: hath he said, and shall he not do it? Or hath he spoken, and shall not make it good? Behold, I have received commandment to bless: and he hath blessed; and I cannot reverse it. If God said it he will do it, believe it He cannot go back on his own word. When you decide to walk with Jesus you might start out in a moan, but when you commit to him, and you trust him at his word your moaning will turn into praise. Don't feel like you are not good enough to come to Jesus he know the gifts that God has place in you. He formed you while you were yet in your mother's womb. He knows your destiny, and your dreams that are within you, that you cannot see. The Holy Spirit of God will help you to unlock what's in you. What person would not want to serve a loving Savior like Jesus? Choose ye this day whom you will serve. Have you made Jesus your choice: If not, who side are you on? Or, what is there in hell you need or want? Amen.

Sin through Adam and Salvation through Christ

In the beginning God created the perfect place for man to inhabit. But along the way woman became deceived and man was persuaded. Thereby bringing sin into a world that was created after the righteousness of God. Our spirit was of God but our flesh was of the dust of the ground. The book of Ephesians (4: 4-6) tells us there is one body, and one Spirit, even as you are called in one hope of your calling. One Lord; one faith, one baptism. One God and father of all, who is above all, and through all, and in you all. According to the book of Genesis God created man in his own image. God breathed the breath of life into man, and man became a living soul. Genesis (1:26-28): And God said, Let us make man in our own image, after our likeness: and let them have dominion over the fish of the sea, and over the fowls of the air, and over cattle, and over all the earth, and over every creeping thing that creepeth upon the earth. God created man and gave them dominion over everything that he had made. And at that time man had no knowledge of what sin was for he was made after God in true righteousness. And God blessed them, and God said unto them, be fruitful, and multiply, and replenish the earth, and subdue it: God blessed them, and gave them a command to increase in the earth, and to have authority over everything. And God said, Behold, I have given you every herb bearing seed, which is upon the face of all the earth, and every tree, in which is the fruit of a tree yielding seed; to you it shall be for meat. God had made provision in everything that man would ever need or want. Genesis (2:8-9): And the Lord God planted a garden eastward in Eden; and he put the man whom he had formed. And out of the ground made the Lord God to grow every tree that is pleasant to the sight, and good for food; the tree of life also in the midst of the garden, and the tree of knowledge of good and evil. God had made every tree in the garden available for man to eat from.

God had given one commandment not to eat from the tree of the knowledge of good and evil. Genesis (2:15-17): And the Lord God took the man, and put him into the Garden of Eden to dress it and to keep it. And the Lord God commanded the man, saying, of every tree of the garden thou mayest freely eat: But of the tree of knowledge of good and evil, thou shalt not eat of it, for in the day that thou eatest thereof thou shalt surely die. God had given commandment that Adam could freely eat of every tree in the garden, except the tree of good and evil. Can you image how many trees were in that garden that was pleasant to be desired? And all God commanded was just leave this one tree alone. God cares about us so much that he wants to make sure all of our needs are met. Philippians (4:19): For my God shall supply all my need according to his riches and glory by Christ Jesus. God knows what our needs are before we ask him. And if we ask in faith we shall receive it. Genesis (2:18) says that God didn't think it was good for man to be alone, so he created Adam a help meet. The Bible says a man that finds a wife finds a good thing. So therefore God caused a deep sleep to fall upon Adam, and God took a rib from man and made woman. Adam called his wife Eve, because she was the mother of every living thing. Genesis (2:25): And they were both naked, the man and his wife, and were not ashamed. Adam and Eve were not ashamed because they knew no sin everything was perfect that God had created. They had no knowledge of good and evil; no knowledge of right and wrong.

They were clothed in the righteousness of God, Gods glory covered their mind, body, and soul. Sin entered into the Garden of Eden by disobedience, and deception.

The book of Genesis tells us that out of all the beast that God had made the serpent was more subtle (cunning, crafty). The serpent approach Eve in the garden, and ask a question. Be, careful always examine questions before giving an answer to make sure they are from the Lord. Genesis (3:1-5): And he said to the woman, Yea, hath God said, ye shall not eat of every tree of the garden? And the woman said unto the serpent, we may eat of the fruit of the trees of the garden: But of the fruit of the tree which is in the midst of the garden, God hath said, ye shall not eat of it, neither shall ye touch it, lest ye die. And the serpent said unto the woman, ye shall not surely die. But do you know that Satan will come to you with a half truth of God word he bends and twists words to make it fix his own lifestyle, but a half truth is a whole lie in the eyesight of God. For God doth know that in the day ye eat thereof, then your eyes shall be opened, and ye shall be as gods, knowing good and evil. Satan will deceive you with things that will appeal to your satisfaction, but Satan deal directly with sin. Satan had deceived Eve into eating from the tree which God had given commandment not to eat, and Eve also persuaded Adam. Therefore sin entered into the world because of their disobedience, and their eyes were opened. The Bible tells us that they knew that they were naked. Adam and Eve heard the voice of God walking in the garden, and hide themselves from the presence of the Lord. Adam told God that they hid because they were naked. Genesis (3:11): And he said, who told thee that thou wast naked? Hast thou eaten of the tree, whereof I commanded thee that thou shuoldest not eat. Then that's where everybody blames one another. (Adam blamed God): Adam said the woman whom thou gavest to be with me, she gave me of the tree and I did eat. (Eve blamed the serpent): saying the serpent beguiled (Deceive) or seduce me, and I did eat.

Genesis (3:14): And the Lord God said unto the serpent, Because thou hast done this, thou art cursed above all cattle, and above every beast of the field; upon thy belly shalt thou go, and dust shalt thou eat all the days of thy life. And God also put a curse upon man, and woman. God told Eve he would greatly multiply her sorrow and her conception in child birth and her desire shall be to her husband only and he shall rule over her. And to Adam he said, because thou have listen to your wife and ate of the tree of knowledge, God said cursed is the ground for thy sake; in sorrow shalt thou eat of it all the days of your life. Adam and Eve didn't have a care in the world, because God had everything provided for them. Now they were in a position where they would have to provide for themselves. God is so gracious that he banished Adam and Eve from the Garden of Eden by putting an Angle with a sword to block them from eating from the tree of life. Had they eaten from the tree of life, man would have lived for ever in a sinful state, with no hope.

Ask yourself a question if Adam and Eve died a spiritual and physical death, which they did. Ask yourself this question if you died today where would you spend eternity? If heaven is your goal then there are four things that you need to know in order to make it there. (1). Romans (3:23): For all have sinned, and come short of the glory of God. Because of the fall of Adam and Eve sin entered into the world, and therefore everyone that is born, is born a sinner. Romans (5:12): Wherefore, as by one man sin entered into the world, and death by sin; and so death passed upon all men, for they all have sinned. The Bible tells us that even if you have not sinned personally, because we are made after the similitude of Adam's transgression, we are sinners by DNA. (2). Romans (6:23): For the wages of sin is death; but the gift of God is eternal life through Jesus Christ our Lord. (3). John (3:16): For God so loved the world that he gave his only begotten son, that whosoever believeth in him should not perish, but have everlasting life.

Our sin has earned a wage. That wage is death, which is an eternal separation from God. Romans (5:15): But not as the offence, so also is the free gift. For if through the offence of one many be dead, much more the grace of God, and the gift by grace, which is by one man, Jesus Christ, hath abounded unto many. Death passed upon many by one man, and life eternal passed to many by Jesus. Romans (5:18): Therefore as by the offence of one judgment came upon all men to condemnation; even so by the righteousness of one the free gift came upon all men unto justification of life. The judgment that we were subject to because of Adam was death, but with Jesus we are justified. Jesus paid our penalty for us, which no other man could do. That's why we must accept Jesus as our Lord and Savior. Jesus was the only man to conquer sin, to defeat death. Romans (6:3): Know ye not, that so many of us as were baptized into Jesus Christ were baptized into his death? Therefore we are buried with him by baptism into his death: that like as Christ was raised from the dead by the glory of the father, even we also should walk in newness of life.

When we accept Jesus we are a new creation. Our outward man doesn't change, but our inwardly man (spirit man) changes. The Bible says be ye transformed by the renewing of your mind. Even if you don't see a change on the outside just know that the inward man is being transformed day by day, when you study the word of God. If you have made Jesus your Lord and Savior you no longer have the DNA of death through Adam, but you now have the DNA of life through Jesus. The gift that God gave us is eternal life through Jesus Christ. So therefore we must receive Jesus in order to receive God's gift of eternal life. (4) Revelation (3:20). Behold, I stand at the door, and knock: if any man hear my voice, and open the door, I will come in to him. Jesus stands at the door of your heart waiting for you to invite him in as savior. So, taking Him as your savior is the next step. How? Simple ask God to save you. Now if you are in Christ Jesus likewise reckon ye also yourselves to be dead indeed unto sin, but alive unto God through Jesus Christ our Lord. Now that you have accepted Jesus you have to make a decision not to let sin govern your life. Romans (6:12): Let not sin therefore reign in your mortal body, that ye should obey it in the lusts thereof. Romans (6:13): Neither yield ye your member as instruments of unrighteousness unto sin: but yield yourself unto God, as those that are alive from the dead, and your members as instruments of righteousness unto God. He said now that your DNA has changed don't heed your body to sin any more, but unto the righteousness of God, use your body to glorified God, and appose sin unto death.

The Bible says that because we are not under the law, but under grace given to us by God through Jesus. Therefore shall sin have no more dominion over you? You have that right as a believer to live according to the grace that has been giving to you, to help you govern your life in righteousness. Romans (6:16): Know you not, that to whom ye yield yourselves servants to obey, his servants ye are to whom to obey; whether of sin unto death, or of obedience unto righteousness. If you yield to the flesh then you will serve the flesh, but if you yield to the word of God you will serve righteousness. Galatians (5:16-25): This I say then, walk in the spirit, and ye shall not fulfill the lust of the flesh. If you walk after the spirit you want fall into the trap of the enemy. Walking in the love of God produces things that are born of righteousness. In doing so your mind is on Jesus and not on the things of the world. For the flesh lusteth against the spirit, and the spirit against the flesh, and these are contrary the one to the other: so ye cannot do the things that ye would. He says that your flesh and your spirit are warring inside against one another. The flesh is fighting to have control, and so is the spirit. You have to take control of whom to follow; if the spirit of God, then seek those thing that are eternal.

If the flesh, then seek those things which are earthly, and temporary. But if ye be led of the spirit, ye are not under the law. The law minds the things that are corrupt, but the spirit minds the things that are incorrupt. Now the works of the flesh are manifest, which are these: Adultery, fornication, uncleanness, lasciviousness: Idolatry, witchcraft, hatred, variance, emulation, wrath, strife, seditions, heresies:

Envyings, murders, drunkenness, revellings, and such like: of which I tell you before, as I have also told you in time past, that they which do such things shall not inherit the kingdom of God. The Bible tells us that God made Abraham the father of many nations, Abraham was blessed in all things, and if ye are in Christ you fall under the blessings of Abraham. Galatians (3:13-14) Christ hath redeemed us from the curse of the law, being made a curse for us: for it is written, cursed is every one that hangeth on a tree: That the blessing of Abraham might come on the Gentiles (Nations) through Jesus Christ; that we might receive the promise of the spirit through faith. The book of Deuteronomy chapter 28, tells us that if we do the commandments of God all his blessing shall come upon us. The Bible also tells us that the earth is the Lord and the fullness thereof; everything belongs to our heavenly father. But the fruit of the spirit is love, joy, longsuffering, gentleness, goodness, faith: Meekness, temperance (self control); against such there is no law.

You don't need a law when you are walking in righteousness, because Gods word cannot be compromised with doing evil or walking after the flesh, (Gods word not Satan's word). You can walk into your inheritance by Following after the fruit of the spirit, because these shall inherit the kingdom of God. And they that are Christ's have crucified the flesh with the affection and lusts. If we live in the spirit, let us also walk in the spirit. Apostle Paul tells us that we must die daily to our flesh, if we are to walk in the spirit, we will not fulfill the desires of the flesh. He says if you are going to live in the spirit, then walk in the spirit also. The book of James says that a double minded man is unstable in all his ways. You cannot be an effective servant of the Lord Jesus if you are trying to be a servant of the devil. You cannot do righteousness with corruptive thinking.

Galatians (6:7-9): Be not deceived; God is not mocked: for whatsoever a man soweth, that shall he also reap. For he that soweth to his flesh shall of the flesh reap corruption; but he that soweth to the spirit shall of the spirit reap life everlasting. And let us not be weary in well doing: for in due season we shall reap, if we faint not. Here he's letting us know that if we just hold on to God's unchanging hand everything will be alright. There is a reward in the victory of Jesus. We don't have to wait until we get to heaven to enjoy what God has for us. For his word says if we seek first the kingdom of God and his righteousness all this things will be added unto you. God said that he shall supply all your need according to his riches and glory by Christ Jesus. And this is the salvation in Jesus Christ everlasting life. Amen.

Walking In the Abundant Of God

Before you were ever conceive in your mother's womb, God had a purpose and a plan for your life. God had already preordained your life he has order your steps. He has laid a foundation for you to follow. In order to find out your gift that has been placed in you, you must hook up to the creator of life, which is the almighty God. Ephesians (1:3): Blessed be the God and father of our Lord Jesus Christ, who hath blessed us with all spiritual blessings in heavenly places in Christ. Our blessings have already been established in heaven, in Jesus our Lord and Savior. As believer's we must learn how to access our heavenly account, just as you would your earthly account, but your heavenly account require faith. Matthew (16:19): And I will give unto thee the keys of the kingdom of heaven: And whatsoever thou shalt bind on earth shall be bound in heaven: And whatsoever thou shalt loose on earth shall be loosed in heaven. God says he has given us the keys to his kingdom; we have permission to access our blessings and to bind up our curses. We can release all the things that are of God, and bind up anything that is of the enemy. God said whatever you do on the earth he will do it in the heavenly.

The Bible tells us that God will open the windows of heaven, and pour out blessings that we have not enough room to receive. But in order to receive the blessings of God we must line up with his word. God has already made provisions on his part. The book of Genesis tells us that God gave dominion to man, but woman was deceived and man was persuaded. But through the grace of God we are redeemed from the curse of the law through the shed blood of Jesus Christ our Lord and Savior. Through Jesus we have access to the blessings of Abraham. Galatians (3:13-14): Christ hath redeemed us from the curse of the law, being made a curse for us: for it is written, cursed is every one that hangeth on a tree: That the blessings of Abraham might come on the Gentiles (Nations) Through Jesus Christ; that we might receive the promise of the spirit through faith. Ephesians (1:5-7): Having predestinated (foreordained) us unto the adoption of children by Jesus Christ to himself, according to the good pleasure of his will. We are adopted into the family of God through Jesus, and as children of the household of God we have an unlimited inherit. In whom we hath redemption through his blood, the forgiveness of sins, according to the riches of his grace. We have been forgiven of our sins through the shed blood of Jesus. Therefore when we go to God in prayer, God sees us through the eyes of his son Jesus. Jesus is our mediator (intercedes for us) God doesn't see our sin he sees our redemption through Christ.

God thinks of us in a way that no one else will, he says in Jeremiah (29:11): For I know the thoughts that I think toward you, saith the Lord, thoughts of peace and not of evil, to give you an expected end. Not only is God interest in supplying all our need according to his riches in glory by Christ Jesus, but he's also interest in us having an abundant ending. Proverbs (3:1-2): My Son, forget not my law but let thine heart keep my commandments: For length of days, and long life, and peace, shall they add to thee. God not only promises to supply our need, but he says also if we keep his commandments in our heart his words will lengthen our life and keep us in perfect peace, if our mind stays on Jesus. Proverbs (3:5-6): Trust in the Lord with all your heart; and lean not unto your own understanding. In all your ways acknowledge him; and he shall direct thy path. God is not only looking to bless us financially, but also mentally, physically, and spiritually. God says that if you embrace his word, and walk therein his word will be health to thy navel, and marrow to thy bones.

God is letting you know that there is also healing for your body in his word. Psalms (103: 2-5): Bless the Lord, O my soul, and forget not all his benefits. Who forgiveth all thine iniquities; who healeth all thy diseases. Who redeemeth thy life from destruction; who crowneth thee with loving-kindness and tender mercies: Who satisfieth thy mouth with good things; so that thy youth is renewed like the eagle's. God has made provisions for everything we need in this life we just have to trust him. The Bible says that every good and perfect gift comes from above. Proverbs (3:9-10): Honor the Lord with thy substance, and with thy fruits of all thine increase. So shall thy barns be filled with plenty, and thy presses shall burst out with new wine. There is a promise in God word, that if you give him the first portion of every area of your life, he will increase you in all. Ephesians (3:20): Now unto him that is able to do exceeding abundantly above all that we ask or think, according to the power that worketh in us. God can do above what our mind is not able to comprehend. 1John (4:4): Ye are of God, little children, and have overcome them, because greater is he that is in you then he that is in the world. There are things in this world that are great, but our God is greater and can defeat anything in this world that comes up against us. Proverbs chapter 3 also tells us not to despise the chastening of the Lord, because the Lord corrects whom he loves. It's an honor to be corrected by the Lord to know that he only wants the best for his children.

For God says in Isaiah (55:8-9, 11): For my thoughts are not your thoughts, neither are you ways my ways, saith the Lord. For as the heavens are higher than the earth, so are my ways higher than your ways, and my thoughts than your thoughts. So shall my word be that goeth forth out of my mouth: it shall not return unto me void, but it shall accomplish that which I please, and it shall prosper in the thing whereto I sent it. God knows about our life, because he created us and purposes a plan for us from the beginning that exceeds our understanding. That's why he says that my thoughts are not your thoughts, and the plans he has for us are to give us an expected end. God sees our beginning, middle and our end. If we allow him to govern our lives he will guide us to the destiny that he has purpose just for us. God had ordained that narrow pathway for us that lead to life everlasting. But without his help we will wander down that wide pathway to destruction. God is looking for a reason to bless us, he wants to run us down with blessing, but it requires obedience, and faith in his word. Malachi (3:10-11): Bring ye all he tithes into the storehouse, that there may be meat in my house, and prove me now herewith, saith the Lord of hosts, if I will not open you the windows of heaven, and pour you out blessing that there shall not be room enough to receive it. God is challenging us to put his household first, and in return trust that if we take care of his house he will take care of ours. God says put me to the test I will open the abundant of heaven and rain into our lives blessing that we do not have room enough to contain. And I will rebuke the devourer (seed eater) for your sake, and he shall not destroy the fruit of your ground; neither shall your vine cast her fruit before the time of the field, saith the Lord of host.

The Lord promised a rebuking of those things that devour our finances, but also other areas as well. God's provides financially for those who faithfully give. God invites people to try him to verify His trustworthiness with their giving. God is looking for obedience he wants us to walk in abundant that's part of our inheritance. By withholding our giving, we rob God of the privilege of pouring out great and overflowing blessings. God lines it up this way first, there should be food or resources for God's work (in my house). Second, He says those who give will be placed in position to receive overflow in blessings. Third, God says that He will "rebuke the devourer" for our sake. Satan himself cannot stop it.

✍ *Obedience is better than sacrifice*

God is asking for obedience and he always rewards obedience. Do not be afraid to trust God with your giving; he is God, and he will not fail. God says that his word will not return void, but it shall accomplish which I please, and it shall proper in the thing whereto I sent it. Proverbs (13:22): A good man leaveth an inheritance to his children's children: and the wealth of the sinner is laid up for the just. We already have a promise from God that the wealth of the sinner is laid up for his children. We are the just, the Bible says that the just shall live by faith. Are you the just and are you living by faith? So we must be patient, God has already ordain the wealth for us. That wealth is about to transfer in the hands of the just. God is not just concerned with our financial need. When Jesus died on the cross he took every sin in life and nailed it to the cross with him. Everything that was under the curse he took and buried it with him. And when he rose on the third day he rose with not just some power, but with all power in heaven and in the earth. Jesus died for our sins, our sicknesses, our diseases, our prosperity, etc. God has made provision for every area in our life.

Isaiah (53:4-5): Surly he hath borne our griefs, and carried our sorrows; yet we did esteem him stricken, smitten of God, and afflicted. But he was wounded for our transgressions he was bruised for our iniquities: the chastisement of our peace was upon him, and with his stripes we are healed. Jesus took upon himself our sins he carried our burdens, our suffering, our sicknesses, both spiritual and physical. He took our wickedness and rebellion, And Jesus did this for all mankind. So whatever you need financially it's already there, whatever you need physically it's there, whatever you need mentally it's already there. God finished his work on the six day and he rested from all his work on the seventh day. Jesus finished his work on the cross when he lifted up his head to God and said it's is finished. The Bible says he gave up the ghost (died). He said father into thy hands I commit my Spirit. Jesus buried sin and left it in the grave; preached to those that were held captive and led them to freedom. Jesus is now at rest on the right hand of his father. Everything is available to us; we just have to access it by faith and the grace that has been given to us by God the father. Rest in the finish work of Jesus, it shouldn't be a struggle to have your needs met.

The Bible says just as Jesus is so are you in this world. 3John (1: 2): Beloved, I wish above all things that thou mayest prosper and be in health, even as thy soul prospereth. In this verse John was interceding for our behalf, he was praying for us physically, materially, emotionally, and spiritually. Sometime when we don't know how to pray, or what to pray, have someone pray for you, and get in agreement with them. Matthew (18:19): Again I say unto you, if two of you shall agree on earth as to touching anything that they shall ask, it shall be done for them of my father which is in heaven. Jesus tells us right here if we ask any thing of his father in heaven it shall be done. Matthew (18:20): For where two or three are gathered in my name, there am I in the midst. So when we are in agreement on our prayer Jesus is right there in the center of it all. Therefore God sees his son standing there interceding on our behalf. That should build up our confidence to know that Jesus cares enough to personally be in the midst of our prayer life. We should always remember that he's always there, not just in our prayer life but in everything. Jesus says that he will never leave us nor for sake us. The Lord loves us so much that he has covered every area of our life. He has laid a foundation for us to be strengthen in weakness.

Isaiah (40:29-31): He giveth power to the faint; and to them that have no might he increaseth strength. But they that wait upon the Lord shall renew their strength; they shall mount up with wings as eagles; they shall run, and not be weary; and they shall walk, and not faint. All we have to do is wait on God, and not be impatient. Sometimes we try and fix things ourselves and God is telling us to wait and see the salvation of the Lord. When we have done all there is to do God says to stand (just stand). Isaiah (54: 17): Say no weapon that is formed against thee shall prosper; and every tongue that shall rise against thee it judgment thou shall condemn. This is the heritage of the servants of the Lord, and their righteousness is of me, saith the Lord. God knows better than we do what we have need of all we have to do is trust in him. If we know dust far that God has provided for us, than we should trust that he will continue. When the disciples ask Jesus how to pray, Jesus told his disciples when you pray enter into your closet, and shut the door. Sometimes when we pray to our heavenly father we have to shut everything and everybody out. And sometimes it's a good idea to keep our prayer between us and the Lord, because people will try and hinder our prayers.

What we pray in secret God will reward openly. Matthew (6:7-10): But when ye pray, use not vain repetitions, (act of repeating) as the heathen (idolater) do: for they think that they shall be heard for their much speaking. Be not therefore like unto them: for your father knoweth what things ye have need of, before ye ask him. Jesus is letting us know that God knows all about our needs, therefore he will not let us go without. When we pray it might not come when we want it, but if we just keep on believing and putting God first our prayer will be on time. After this manner therefore pray ye: Our Father which art in heaven, Hallowed (sanctify) be thy name. Thy kingdom come, Thy will be done in earth, as it in heaven. God wants his children to have everything that's in heaven on the earth. We done have to wait to we get to heaven to be blessed with the abundant of God. We don't have to wait to have our healing, our joy, our peace, love, wealth, protection we can have that all right here. 1Samuel chapter 15 tells us that to obey is better than sacrifice.

God rewards those that are obedient, and faithful to his word. Examples: Of two different women in 2Kings Chapter 4. One was obedient to the instructions that were given to her by the man of God. The other one took care of the man of God (Elisha) and they were rewarded by God for their and obedience. 2Kings (4:1-7): (Paraphrased) There cried a certain woman she told Elisha that thy servant my husband is dead. She told him that the creditor wanted to take her two sons to be bondmen to pay off the debt. Elisha asked her what she had in her house. She said only a pot of oil. Elisha told her to borrow as many empty vessels as she could. Then he told the woman to take her two sons and go in the house and shut the door behind them, and pour the oil into the empty vessels: The woman did as Elisha had instructed her to do. She began to pour the oil, and as long as she had an empty vessel the oil kept flowing. When there were no more empty vessels the Bible says the oil stayed (stopped). And that's how the abundant of God want to operate in your life. Then she told Elisha everything that happened. Elisha told her to go and sell the oil and pay off the debt, and live you and your sons off the rest. 2Kings (4:8-37): (Paraphrased). This fell on a day that Elisha passed to Shunem. The Bible calls her a great woman, offered Elisha some bread to eat. As often as Elisha passed through Shunem, he ate at the house of this woman. The woman told her husband that she believed that Elisha was a Holy man.

She ask her husband let's make him a chamber on the wall and put a bed, and a table, and a stool, and a candlestick in the room. She told her husband that whenever he comes to Shunem he will have a place to stay. The woman and her husband took care of the man of God. Elisha laid in the chamber thinking, and he said to Gehazi, his servant; call the Shunammite woman. When the woman came before Elisha, he told her you have taking such good care of us, Elisha ask her what can I do for you? Elisha offered to speak to the king or the captain of the host for her, and she told him that she dwell among her own people. Elisha wanted to do something to bless her, so he asks Gehazi, his servant, what can be done for the Shunammite woman? Gehazi, his servant, told Elisha that she has no children, and her husband is old. Elisha, called for the woman, and told her that according to the time of life she would conceive a son. The woman told Elisha, no my Lord don't lie to me. The woman conceived, and had a son at the season that Elisha had told her. When the child grew up he was out reaping with his father, and grabs his head. The father told the servant to take the boy to his mother, the mother held her child until noon, and the child died. She went and laid the child on the bed of Elisha. The woman call for the servant, and told him to get one of the asses and drive her to the man of God. She told him to go fast as he could unless she told him otherwise. Elisha seen the woman coming, and told Gehazi to go and meet her and ask if everything is well with her, her husband and her child, she responded everything is well.

When she came to Elisha, she fell at his feet. Gehazi went to stop her, but Elisha told him to leave her alone; for her soul is troubled, and the Lord has hid it from him. The woman ask Elisha, did I ask you for a son, did I not say don't deceived me? He told Gehazi to go and lay his staff upon the child. He told him don't stop to talk to anyone, and don't get detracted. Elisha went in and seen that the child was died, he shut the door and prayed to the Lord. Elisha lay upon the child, and put his mouth upon his mouth, his eyes upon his eyes, his hands upon his hands, and the child's flesh became warm. Elisha walked back and forth, than stretched himself upon the child. And the Bible says that the child sneezed seven times and opened his eyes. He gave the child back to his mother. When God blesses you nothing and no one can take your blessing from you, not even Satan himself. The woman took care of the man of God, and God rewarded her by blessing her with a son. She didn't ask for anything, but God knew what she had need of. That's what God does for his children. He is a God that sits high and looks low. God is a God of more than enough. It's not just about wealth, but he wants nothing missing in your life, nothing broken, and no one hurting.

And when your journey is over here it's not the end it's just the beginning. Revelation (21:3-7) And I heard a great voice out of heaven saying, Behold, the tabernacle of God is with men, and he will dwell with them, and they shall be his people, and God himself shall be with them, and be their God. And God shall wipe away all tears from their eyes; and there shall be no more death, neither, sorrow, nor crying, neither shall there be any more pain, for the former things are passed. When we get to heaven we are going to experience love like we have never experience before. No more crying, no sickness, on lack, no pain, only fulfillment. And he that sat upon the throne said, Behold, I make all things new. He said unto me, Write: for these words are true and faithful. And he said unto me I am Alpha and Omega, the beginning and the end I will give unto him that is athirst of the fountain of water of life freely. He that overcometh shall inherit all things; I will be his God, and he shall be my son. And we will ever be with the Lord. Amen.

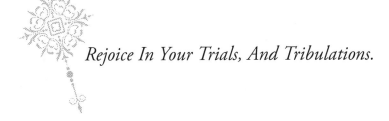

Rejoice In Your Trials, And Tribulations.

James chapter (1:2-4): My brethren, count it all joy when ye fall into divers temptations (various trials); verse 3—Knowing this, that the trying of your faith worketh patience. James is letting you know that in this life, your trials and tribulations are coming to help develop you. To help you learn to wait on the Lord. A lot of times we feel as though God is not answering our prayers, because we don't see the results right away. We have to be mindful and have confidence that God has answered our prayers; God's timing is perfect he's not on our timing. As long as we live in this physical world there are going to be trials and tribulations. When trials come rejoice because they are helping us to grow, and to be ready for the next one that's sure to follow: We are developing patience in the things of God. Anything that has not been tested has not been approved. If we are not been tested we are not growing, we are still as a baby being feed with milk. We don't want to be stagnated in the same area. When trials do come rejoice, knowing that our heavenly father has already brought us through, and is able to do it again: But let patience have her perfect work, that you may be perfect and entire, wanting nothing. We are developing moral, and spiritual growth, we are not rejoicing in the trials it's self, but in the possible results. Our trials serve as a way of stripping away any thing that is false.

Patience is a positive steadfastness that bravely endures. When he is talking about perfect works, he's saying, not that you might be sinless, but the thought of fullness and wholeness. God wants us wealth, it's not just about money. Yes we need money to live, to get the gospel out all over the world. Wealth from God means nothing missing in your life, nothing broken in your life, and no one hurting. Trials are hardships that are meant to try your faith. 2Corinthians (1:3-4): Blessed be the God and father of our Lord Jesus Christ, the father of mercies and God of all comfort: Who comforts us in all our tribulation, that we might be able to comfort those who are in any trouble, with the comfort which we ourselves are comforted by God. Paul is letting us know what ever hardships we go through God Is right there to comfort us. 2Corinthians (12:9): And he said unto me, my grace is sufficient for thee: for my strength is made perfect in weakness. 2Corinthians (4: 8-9): We are troubled on every side, yet not distressed; we are perplexed, but not in despair: Persecuted, but not forsaken; cast down, but not destroyed. Just know that when your trials and tribulations feel as though they have broken you down, or weaken you God said that his grace is sufficient. His grace is able to take care of all area in our life.

God said to cast all your cares upon him for he cares for you. If we just hold on to God in our trials and tribulations he will bring us through the fire. Psalm (66: 10-12): For thou, O God hast proved us: thou hast tried us, as sliver is tried. Thou broughtest us into the net; thou laidst affliction upon our loins. Thou hast caused men to ride over our heads; we went through fire and through water: but thou broughtest us out into a wealthy place. When we endure the fire and the water we come out as perfection. Jesus does not leave us when we go through our trials and tribulations, he right there. Jesus tells us in his word, I will never leave you nor for sake you. We all have trials and tribulations, but the different between us and the world is we go through, because we have the Holy Spirit to guide us. The world stays in them, because they have no one to show or to lead them out.

Not only do we have hope, but we have faith in Jesus. Matthew (11:28-30): Jesus said come unto me, all ye that labor and are heavy laden, and I will give you rest, in that rest is a rest form everything that troubles us. Our trials may come from our family life, our jobs, our health, our husband or wife, but Jesus said you can rest from all that if you learn to give it to him. Take my yoke upon you, and learn of me; for I am meek and lowly in heart: and ye shall find rest unto your souls. For my yoke is easy, and my burden is light: If we take upon the mind set of Jesus, and trust in him we can relax when afflictions come. Because Jesus is a burden barrier, a mind regulator, he mends the broken heart and lift up bowed down heads. The Bible tells us just as Jesus is so are we in this world so if Jesus yoke is easy and his burden light so are ours in this world. God never said that it would be easy, but he said let not your heart be trouble. John (14:1-3): Let not your heart be troubled: ye believe in God, believe also in me. In my father's house are many mansions: if it were not so, I would have told you. I go to prepare a place for you. And if I go and prepare a place for you, I will come again, and receive you unto myself; that where I am, there ye may be also. Jesus was given us words of comfort to let us know that there is a reward after you have endured this life. It is only for a moment, but with him on our side we are more than conquerors. Jesus says in John (14:27): Peace I leave with you, my peace I give unto you: not as the world giveth, give I unto you. Let not your heart be troubled, neither let it be afraid. When trials and tribulations come our way learn to rest in the peace of Jesus, just like Jesus rested in the peace of his father. When Jesus was doing the will of the father he was in rest no matter what came against him, he has that faith that his father would deliver him. When we are doing the work of the Lord, we should have that same faith that Jesus had in God to know that he will deliver us.

God has already prepared a way of escape; he said in his word that he would not put upon you more than you are able to bear. Thessalonians (3: 3-4): That no man should be moved by these afflictions: for yourselves know that we are appointed thereunto. He's says that this shouldn't come as a surprise, Jesus have already foretold us that in this life we would have tribulation. John (16:33): These things I have spoken unto you, that in me ye might have peace. In the world ye shall have tribulation: but be of good cheer; I have overcome the world. Jesus is saying there is always peace in him, but even in the world we can still have peace if we keep our mind stayed on him. We can go through our trials and tribulations with joy knowing that Jesus has overcome the world. In Jesus we can do all things if we pick up our cross and follower him. In weakness, Philippians (4:13) say I can do all things through Christ which strengtheneth me.

The Bible says that ye are of God, little children, and have overcome them: because greater is he that is in you, then he that is in the world. Don't be fearful when trials and tribulations come because we have access by faith into this grace wherein we stand, and rejoice in the hope of the glory of God. But seek ye first the kingdom of God and all of his righteousness and everything else will be added unto you. In other words if we pray and have faith in Jesus we can ask what we will in his name and that he will do, so that the father will be glorified in the Son. Prayer is the key to the kingdom and faith unlock the door to kingdom of heaven. Romans (5:3-6): And not only so, but we glory in tribulations also: knowing that tribulation worketh patience: And patience, experience; and experience, hope: And hope maketh not ashamed; because the love of God is shed abroad in our hearts by the Holy Ghost which is given unto us.

◈ *God's plan for redemption*

For when we were yet without strength, in due time Christ died for the ungodly. God had a plan for us sense the beginning of creation. A plan and an appointed time where we would need a savior that would strength us in our most weaken state. Jesus was our example he came in the form of a fleshly body and endured trials and tribulations just as we do. Jesus showed us that in our weakness we are made strong through him, that we can endure hardship as a good soldier. 1Peter: (4:1): FORASMUCH then as Christ hath suffered for us in the flesh, arm yourselves likewise with the same mind: For he that hath suffered in the flesh hath ceased from sin. He says when we have suffered in the flesh we have ceased from sin, because we are not walking in the flesh anymore, we are now walking in the spirit. The Bible says if you walk in the spirit you shall not fulfill the lust of the flesh. 1Peter (4: 12-16): Beloved, think it not strange concerning the fiery trials which is to try you, as though some strange thing happened unto you. If through the fiery trials let your life witness for Jesus, regardless of circumstances. But rejoice, inasmuch as ye are partakers of Christ's sufferings; that, when his glory shall be revealed, ye may be glad also with exceeding joy. We need to understand that suffering is part of being a Christian if you are to walk with Jesus. God expects us to live godly, even in the midst of trials, suffering, or persecution. If ye be reproached for the name of Christ, happy are ye; for the spirit of glory and of God resteth upon you: on their part he is evil spoken of, but on your part he is glorified. Our circumstance should not affect godly living on our part. If we can still follow Jesus in the midst of our trials God will be glorified in us to the world, that's a testimony in its self.

But let none of you suffer as a murderer, or as a thief, or as an evildoer, or a busybody in other men's matters. In this life you will have trials and tribulations, which mean we, will go through some suffering in our life. So if you suffer for righteousness sake, God said that he will reward you for your righteousness. If any man suffer as a Christian, let him not be ashamed; but let him glorify God on this behalf.

Whether we will be embraced or persecuted, our life and testimony are to witness to the hope of salvation in Jesus Christ. Consistency in godly living, despite our trials and tribulations, or our circumstances, it is the true test of growth in godliness. The book of Job tells us how Job went through trials, tribulations, suffering, persecution, hardships, how he lost his children his wealth, and sickness came upon him, but through it all Job still walked in godliness. Job (13:15): Though he slay me, yet will I trust in him: but I will maintain mine own ways before him. Job endured he did not allow his circumstances too out way his trust that God would pull him through. And God blessed Job exceedingly abundantly above all that he could ask or think. Just hold on to God's unchanging hand and everything will be alright. The Bible tells us that weeping may endure for a night, but joy cometh in the morning. When looking at the book of Job, God allowed Job to be tested, Job had fear in him and God knew that Job had to be purged out. God sees in us what we can't see in ourselves, so therefore God uses the enemy to bring us into perfection; He knew what Job was able to handle and he also knows what we can bear. God will not give us something to do that he has not equipped us for. God will not put on you what you are not able to bear, but when trials and tribulations come he has already prepared away of escape.

❧ *Nothing should separate us from the love of God*

Romans (8:35-39): Who shall separate us from the love of Christ? Shall tribulations, or distress, or persecution, or famine, or nakedness, or peril, or sword? Nothing should be able to separate you from the love of God, because it's in him we move, breath, and have our being. As it is written, for thy sake we are killed all the daylong; we are accounted as sheep for the slaughter. When we didn't have Jesus in our lives we were without hope, in Jesus we have salvation. Nay; in all these things we are more than conquerors through him that loved us. You can do anything with Christ on your side he is more than the world can be against you. For I am persuaded, that neither death, nor life, nor angels, nor principalities, nor powers, nor things present, nor things to come: Nor height. Nor depth, any other creature, shall be able to separate us from the love of God, which is in Christ Jesus our Lord. Jesus took upon himself sin that were not his own, he died in our place to give us eternal life.

Why should it be hard for us to endure the things we go through, but for a moment Knowing that the trying of our trials and tribulations is working in you perfection? Matthew (5:10): Blessed are they which are persecuted for righteousness sake: for theirs is the kingdom of heaven. We shall receive a crown of life if we faint not. When our trials and tribulations come look to the hills from which cometh our help, all our help comes from the Lord. Put on the whole armor of God that you may be able to endure, and when you have done all that you can do just call on the name of Jesus he is there for you. Have you notice the four steps we are dealing with as an over comer of our trials and tribulations. The first step is that we must have hope in God. Step two we must trust in God. Step three we must believe that God able to do all things but fail. Step four we must have faith in God that he will work through our trials and tribulations. Amen.

Where Will You Spend Eternity?

There is so much violence in our world today and we just continue to go on about our daily lives like there is nothing we can do. This is not just a call to those that have committed their lives to our Lord and Savior Jesus Christ, but also to people that have not may a decision to commit to making Jesus Lord of their lives. Some children are being raised by the streets instead of being raised by the parents. Ephesians (6:1-4): Children, obey your parents in the Lord: for this is right. God is instructing our children on how to listen to the instructions of their parents. When God created Adam and Eve he placed Adam as the head of the family. Man was place in leadership to be a provider, a protector, to set up rules that were to govern family structure; that would allow the family to run under the order in which God ordained it to be. The husband also has a head over him which is the Lord Jesus Christ. God always run his kingdom in order and in righteousness, his will is to be done. Matthew (6:10): Thy kingdom come; Thy will be done in earth, as it is in heaven. Honor thy father and mother; which is the first commandment with promise. God says that children should respect their parent at all times. God does not see what we see when it comes to honoring parents, there is no stipulations in Gods eyes as to why you should dishonor your parents. We look at excuses as to why we feel like it is ok to dishonor our parents: Examples— some may have parents that are, drug users, alcoholic, abusive mentally, physically, and sexually, molesters, some have even killed their children and to us those are valid reason to not honor or respect our parents. We must always remember no matter what happens in this world God is still on the throne, he is still in charge.

We may never understand why God allows bad things to happen to us, but his word say that he rains on the just and the unjust, God is no respect of person. God does not want us to handle things ourselves he want us to trust in him to take care of our situations. Regardless of how our parents are they or still our parents, and God still wants us to respect them. Psalms (27:10): When my father and my mother forsake me, then the Lord, will take me up. Psalms (27:14): Wait on the Lord: be of good courage, and he shall strengthen thine heart: wait, I say, wait on the Lord. All we have to do is wait, and trust in the almighty God, he is well able to take care of us. Everything that happen God has a purpose and a plan. Ephesians (6: 3-4): That it may be well with thee, and thou mayest live long on the earth. God has made us a promise that he would give us long life if we obey his commandment to honor our parent. No matter what our parents do are how they treat us they are still our parents. Just like we have to give an account to the Lord, our parents also have to give an account to the Lord. And, ye father, provoke not your children to wrath (anger): but bring them up in the nurture and admonition of the Lord. Here he tells the parent not to stir up anger purposely in their children, but to take care of, TRAIN, FEED, NOURISH, EDUCATE, and FORSTER them in the word and the will of God. Parents also have a commandment from the Lord on how they should be responsible for raising their children according to Gods instructions, also to warn gently, reprove with a warning, chide, reproach, rebuke, reprimand and to do so unto love. There are consequents for both the parents and the children for not obeying Gods commands.

Proverbs (22:6): Train up a child in the way he should go: and when he is old, he will not depart from it. The problem we have today is we are not raising our children in the way of God. We the parents are to be examples for our children to follow just as we are to follow after

Christ Jesus. As parents we shouldn't have to drop our children off at the door of the church we should take them to church with us. If we do not raise our children they are going to be raised by the streets. The Bible says that Satan is the prince of this world, so we can either keep them in the hands of God or place them in the hands of the enemy. We are losing our children to the enemy because we have turn from our first love which is the Lord Jesus Christ. And family has taking a back seat in our lives because we have become so busy with the cares of this materialistic world. Our jobs, houses, cars, money and clothes have become our number one reason for living. The structures of family value which our nation was founded upon; that prayer changes things have lost all its meaning to us. God says to cast all our cares upon him because he cares for us. If we trusted in the almighty God we could rest in him. And not have to compromise what's important to God which is family. God created families to be united and not separated. The things that are happening in this world today should make us take notice that the Bible is being fulfilled. We need to take notice that everything that the word of God says is coming to pass. This should be a wakeup call for you to make a decision on where will you spend eternity? You have two choices Jesus or Satan, Heaven or Hell, there is no in between.

People believe in heaven, but most do not believe in hell. Matthew (25:41): Then shall he say also unto them on the left hand, Depart from me, ye cursed, into everlasting fire, prepared for the devil and his angels. Hell was not created for us it was created for Satan and his fallen angels. But not accepting Jesus as our Lord and Savior we have made a choice to reserve a place there for us, and the Bible says hell has enlarged itself. When our physical body dies it goes back to the dust and our spirit departs to wait for its final judgment. If we have not make a choice before we die, it will be to late our rights will be taking away and a choice will be made for us. When we die having never made Jesus our choice than hell has a legal right to us. Some people say that an all loving God would not send us to hell, and you would be right. God does not send us to hell we make the choice ourselves by not accepting Jesus and living accordingly to his will. Jesus died and took our place in hell so we didn't have to go. If we don't accept Jesus, than we must face the torments of hell for ourselves. God gave us free will and he will not interfere with our choice we choose to make. God loves us unconditionally and he will not force his children to be where they do not want to be. God will not force his love upon us he wants us to willingly accepted him. Matthew (25:46): And these shall go away into everlasting punishment: but the righteous into life eternal. The ones that have accepted Jesus are the righteous they will inherit the kingdom of God.

✒ *There shall be weeping and gnashing of teeth.*

The righteous shall for ever be in the presence of the Lord. Where will you spend eternity? Revelation (21:7-8): He that overcometh shall inherit all things; and I will be his God, and he shall be my son. God tells us that if we have made a choice to accept Jesus as Lord of our lives, and endure to the end he shall be a father to us and we shall be his children. And with that in mind we know that a father takes care of his children. But the fearful, and unbelieving, and the abominable (very hateful), and murderers, and whoremongers, and sorcerers, and idolaters (worship of idols, false gods), and all liars, shall have their part in the lake which burneth with fire and brimstone: which is the second death. God says the fearful, and unbelieving will not inherit his kingdom or eternal life but will be cast into eternal darkness, Matthew (8:11-12): And I say unto you: That many shall come from the east and west, and shall sit down with Abraham, and Isaac, and Jacob, in the kingdom of heaven. But the children of the kingdom shall be cast out into outer darkness: there shall be weeping and gnashing of teeth. He talks here about the children of the kingdom but we must look a little deeper into this scripture, a lot of people that call themselves Christians lack faith in God word and in his will. We say that Jesus is Lord of our lives with our mouth but yet we do not have a relationship with him. Never Spend any time with him in fellowship, never turn from the world, but we say he is Lord of our lives. How can we say Jesus is our Lord and we do not know him? We made a confession with our mouth and it never took root in our heart, so that confession was in vain? Our mouth says one thing but our heart is far from him.

We need to examines ourselves and make sure that when we stand before the Lord that he want say depart from me I never knew you. We want to hear well done thou good and faithful servant. Matthews (8:20-23): Wherefore by their fruits ye shall know them. Not everyone that saith unto me, Lord, Lord, shall enter into the kingdom of heaven; but he that doeth the will of my father which is in heaven.

Many shall say to me in that day, Lord, Lord, have we not prophesied in thy name? And in thy name have cast out devils? And in thy name done many wonderful works? And then will I profess unto them, I never knew you: depart from me, ye that work iniquity. The response of Jesus in these scriptures stresses the urgency of truly following him, we can fool people, but we cannot fool the Lord. God sees what's in our heart, and he knows what we will do before we do it. Don't think that we can stand before the Lord on judgment day and talk our way into heaven. God has been knocking on the door of our hearts trying to get us to let him come in and be Lord of our lives. Remember we can't get to the father but by Jesus.

Matthew (7:13-14): Enter ye in at the strait gate: for wide is the gate, broad is the way that leadeth to destruction, and many there be which go in thereat (by it). Jesus says that the wide gate leads to the world and all the lust of the world. The wide gate represents walking in the flesh, and the fleshly body does not operate in the things of God. The only way to operate in the things of God is by walking in the spirit. The Bible says walking in the spirit and you shall not fulfill the lust of the flesh. That's why we must may a decision not to enter into the wide gate, because there are so many rooms to venture into when the gate is wide and broad. Too many ways to turn away from the direction of Jesus, to many distracted on our journey when our eyes should remain on Jesus. The only way to keep our focus on the Lord is by enter the narrow gate.

Because strait is the gate, and narrow is the way, which leadeth unto life, and few there be that find it. That narrow gate represents Jesus the door way to eternal life.

Jesus says few find's it because we tend to look always from our savior instead of keeping our eyes on him. We are in the world, but we are not of the world, the Lord says come from among them be ye separate. When looking at Peter one of the Lords disciple, he accomplished something amazing when looking at Jesus. Peter was looking at that narrow gate. The Bible tells us that Jesus commanded his disciples to get in the ship and go to the other side, while he sent the multitudes away, after having feed them. Matthew (14:24-31) reads: But the ship was now in the midst of the sea, tossed with waves: for the wind was contrary (out of control). And in the fourth watch of the night Jesus went unto them, walking on the sea. 26 And when the disciples saw him walking on the sea, they were troubled, saying: It is a spirit; and they cried out for fear. But straightway Jesus spake unto them, saying: Be of good cheer; is it I; be not afraid. And Peter answered him and said, Lord, if it be thou; bid me come unto thee on the water. And he said, come. And when Peter was come down out of the ship, he walked on the water, to go to Jesus. But when he saw wind boisterous, he was afraid; and beginning to sink, he cried, saying, Lord, save me. And immediately Jesus stretched forth his hand, and caught him, and said unto him, O thou of little faith, wherefore didst thou doubt? You see the concluding facture is that Jesus is that narrow gate that we must enter by, Peter entered and got detracted by the way of the wide gate and fell. Just as we do, he took his eyes of the narrow way only for a moment.

That's why Jesus says that there are few that find it, because we allow the cares of the world to take our mind of Jesus. When he clearly says in his word I am the way, the truth, and the life. And no one can enter in but by me, there is no other way, don't let people fool you into thinking that there is other means by which you can get to heaven. We should never think that because we have done good deeds, have help people or tell ourselves I am a good person that alone should get us into heaven. If so we should ask ourselves the question by whom standards are we judging ourselves on. Ephesians (2:8): States, for by grace are ye saved through faith: and that not of yourselves: it is the gift of God: (9) not of works, lest any man should boast. The word clearly states that we cannot be saved by our works. Therefore no amount of works or good deeds can get us into heaven. It's a free gift from God for us to accept or to turn down. If a gift is the only way to enter heaven and we don't accept that gift; then we have turned down our only means of entering, which is his son Jesus Christ. Romans (14: 11-12): For it is written, as I live, saith the Lord, every knee shall bow to me, and every tongue shall confess to God. There is no other way; God has taken away our excuses we can't confess that we did not know the only way is through Jesus. Because we have his written word, Jesus left us a will. And if we turn it down or waited too long to make our decision thinking we had all the time in the world, what then.

The Bible says no man knows the day nor the hour. (Verse 12): So then every one of us shall give account of himself to God. Our leaders, our parents, our children, no one can answer for us as to why we never chose to may Jesus our choice. The only one who was prefect, the only one that conquered sin; the free gift that was given to all mankind. Through the fall of Adam sin enter into the world, therefore everyone that is born into the world carries that contaminated blood of Adam. Therefore we must be adopted into the family of God through the uncontaminated blood of Jesus by accepting him as our Lord and Savior. How can anyone turn down such a wonderful gift? WHERE WILL YOU SPEND ETERNITY? Make your choice before it too late. Jude: Now unto him that is able to keep you from falling, and to present you faultless before the presence of his glory with exceeding joy, to the only wise God our Savior, be glory and majesty, dominion and power, both now and ever. Amen. *

No Man Knows The Day Or The Hour Of Christ Return.

The Bible teaches that when Jesus ascended into heaven he said that he would return for his bride, which is the body of Christ (The church). John (14: 3): And if I go and prepare a place for you, I will come again, and receive you unto myself; that where I am, there ye may be also. Jesus states that he is going to get our new home ready, and will come at a time that God has appointed for his return. 1 Thessalonians (5:1-2): But of the times and the seasons, brethren, ye have no need that I write unto you. For yourselves know perfectly that the day of the Lord so cometh as a thief in the night. We never expect a thief to make an announcement as to when he's going to break into our homes. Paul compares the coming of Jesus as a thief in the night therefore letting us know that the world will be caught off guard. But the Lord did tell the righteous how to discern certain things that will take place before his return. 2Timothy (3:1-4): This, know also that in the last days perilous (dangerous) times shall comes. For men shall be lovers of their selves, covetous, boasters, proud, blasphemers, disobedient to parents, unthankful, unholy: Without natural affection, trucebreakers, false accusers, incontinent, fierce, despisers of those that are good: Traitors, heady, high-minded, lovers of pleasures more than lovers of God.

Paul is showing us that in the last days, the time from first appearing of Christ until second coming which is referred to in the book of Acts (2:17-21): And it shall come to pass in the last days, says God, That I will pour out My spirit on all flesh; Your sons and your daughters shall prophesy, Your young men shall see visions, Your old men shall dream dreams. And on My menservants and on my maidservants I will pour out my spirit in those days; and they shall prophesy. I will show wonders in heaven above: And signs in the earth beneath: Blood and fire and vapor of smoke. The sun shall be turned into darkness, and the moon into blood: Before the coming of the great and awesome day of the Lord. And it shall come to pass, that whoever shall call on the name of the Lord shall be saved. Everything that the Bible says must come to pass before the return of Jesus, is already being fulfilled. We have heard people saying this have been happening since the beginning of time. But look at the world today how rapidly things are happening now. The season has gotten to a point of when it is suppose to be winter we have hot days, and rainy days. In the summer we have cold days, hurricanes and tornados happening in device places as if the balance of nature has shifted. Therefore making it almost important to tell when it is winter, spring, summer, or fall. Children killing parents, parents killing children, people being raped, and molested without thought. Rob for not only their money, but also for their shoes and clothing. Abused, no respect for any one, breaking in homes, in cars, selling drugs on the street corners, abusing alcohol, prescription medicine, all kinds of lasciviousness (lustfulness) greediness, will kill you for a dollar because life has no value to them.

Homosexuality (men in love with men, and women in love with women and very few preacher will preach on it because of a fear of running a dollar out the door. Clearly the word of God says that it is not good for man to be alone. God said I will make him a help meet, so God created Adam and Eve. God said to Adam and Eve, be fruitful and multiply, that means in the fruit of their bodies to replenish the earth. Genesis (1:27-28): So God created man in his own image, in the image of God created he him; (male and female created he them. And

God blessed them, and God said unto them, be fruitful, and multiply, and replenish the earth.

There is so much corruption in the world running through our world leaders as well as our leaders in Gods house. Marriages among the world are lasted longer than the marriages among Christians. People are living together outside of wed lock, when God says that he sanctified marriage, that it is a covenant between God, the husband, and his wife. Adultery, fornication, backbiting, pridefulness, envying, strife, hatred, Idolatry these things are in the world; which is the work of the wicked one (the devil) and the evidence of the ladder day are upon us. We are so busy until we are not looking at the signs that Jesus said would occur, wars and rumors of war. All this is taking place right in front of our faces and we act as if we have all the time in the world to get our lives together and we don't realize time is running out. We need to look to the hill from which cometh our help. The Bible says that all our help comes from the Lord. The reason these things are happening more rapidly now is because Satan knows time is waning down so he has stepped up his game, And if we do not take notice we will be the ones caught with our work undone. The Lord gave us signs because he love us and don't want any to perish, but that all should come to repentance. The world comes together when tragedy strikes. We run to the church when there is chaos in the world, but only for a moment and then we go back to our daily live.

Matthew (24: 3-7): And as he sat upon the Mount of Olives, the disciples came unto him privately, saying, tell us, when shall these things be? And what shall be the signs of thy coming, and of the end of the world? And Jesus answered and said unto them, Take heed that no man deceive you. For many shall come in my name, saying, I am Christ; and shall deceive many. In this Jesus is letting us know up front to be watchful of those that will come to us in sheep clothing. Beware of false prophets, and pretender's trying to inmate him. But if we don't know what the word of God says we will be the ones falling for an imitation. The Bible says to study to show you approved. The Lord said that my people perish for a lack of knowledge. And ye shall hear of wars and rumors of war: see that ye be not troubled: for all these things must come to pass, but the end is not yet. When any one has giving his life to Jesus there is no need to be troubled. The Bible says that to be absent from the body is to be present with the Lord. And that is our purpose to forever be with the Lord in heavenly places. The news always tells of wars that are happening all over the world right now. Everything that God has spoken is being fulfilled; how can anyone have doubts about the Bible. For nation shall rise against nations, and kingdom against kingdom: and there shall be famines, and pestilences, and earthquakes, in diver's places. Every day there are new diseases spreading all over the world, most of which they can't find a cure. And some are being studied to find out what they are, and as soon as they get a handle on one then there arises another.

Earthquakes are happening in place that even the scientist can't give reasons why they are moving in area that they should not be in. When all they had to do was read the word of God. 1Corinthians (1:27) Read: But God hath chosen the foolish things of the world to confound the wise; and God hath chosen the weak things of the world to confound the things which are mighty. Matt. (24: 29) that no flesh should glory in his presence. God only allows us to discerner certain things, he gives us what he wants us to know, and he will not allow us to figure out what's going to happen before his appointed time. There are people in the world today that says the Bible is in coded.

That may be true, but God will not enlighten us to the things that he has preordained until they have fully come to past. Some people in this world think that there's no God that we just evolved. But yet they can't explain how everything that the word of God says is coming to pass. Matt. (24:8-14) All these are the beginning of sorrows. Things are escalating more and more to where it seemed as if it was year to year, but now it seems as if minute to minute. Soon as one year passes we blink our eyes and there passes another. We can't turn on the news without hearing of some one's life that has been taken by another. We hear a brief moment of something positive and the rest of the story goes downhill from there, not just in the United States, but all over the world. When this verse speaks of the beginning of sorrows it paints a picture of marking the transition from this age to the age to come. (9) Then shall they deliver you up to be afflicted, and shall kill you: and ye shall be hated of the nations for my name's sake. Right now people in other countries are being killed just for calling on the name of Jesus, or even carrying a Bible. People are being hated and abused because of their belief in Jesus, they acknowledge God but they try and exclude his son, our Lord and Savior Jesus Christ. (10) And then shall many be offended, and shall betray one another, and shall hate one another. (11) Then many false prophets will rise up and deceive many. (12) And because lawlessness will abound, the love of many will grow cold. (13) But he who endures to the end shall be saved. (14) And this gospel of the kingdom will be preached in the entire world as a witness to all nations, and then the end will come.

During this time there will be religious deception, social and political upheavals (a violent agitation or change), natural calamities, disloyalty, and persecution all of which are precursors (forerunners) of the end times. In the midst of the difficulties, the Lord's followers are to persevere in spreading the gospel. When viewing our T.V. stations, who can say that the gospel has not been preached to every person, we have net-works like T.B.N. and Day Star and others that are now broadcasting all around the world. Jesus says when all nations have been witnessed to then shall the end come. He did not say everyone had to accept just that they have to be witness to. Matt. (24:16-22) Then let those who are in Judea flee to the mountains. (17) Let him who is on the housetop not go down to take anything out of his house. (18) And let him who is in the field not go back to get his clothes. (19) But woe to those who are pregnant and to those who are nursing babies in those days! (20) And pray that your flight may not be in the winter or on the Sabbath. Jesus gives sound advice to flee the city before escape is impossible he lets them know not to worry about taken any thing with them at this point it would be of no value any way.

Just as the angels of God did when they instructed Lot and his family to get out of Sodom and Gomorrah before the city was to be destroyed, Jesus was also advising them. The Lord always takes care of his people all we need to do is just heed his voice. The Lord says that my sheep hears my voice and the voice of a stranger they will not hear. (21) For then shall be great tribulation, such as was not since the beginning of the world to this time, no, nor ever shall be. (22) And except those days should be shortened, there should no flesh be saved: but for the elect's sake those days shall be shortened. The Lord was letting us know that the times are going to be more horrifying then we could ever image. He tells us that the things that will come upon the world have never been like this since the beginning of creation.

The Lord will not allow us to destroy ourselves.

If the Lord were to allow the time of the world to linger we would eventually destroy one another. And no flesh would be saved, but because of his mercy and grace and the love for his chosen people he will allow our days to be shortened. Matt. (24:23-30) Then if any man shall say unto you, Lo, here is Christ, or there; believe it not. (24) For there shall arise false Christ, and false prophets, and shall shew great signs and wonders; insomuch that, if it were possible, they shall deceive the very elect. (25) Behold, I have told you before. (26) Wherefore if they shall say unto you, Behold, he is in the desert; go not forth: behold, he is in the secret chambers; believe it not. (27) For as the lightning cometh out of the east, and shineth even unto the west; so shall also the coming of the Son of man be. Well taught followers of Jesus will not be deceived by bogus deliverers, but will await the coming of the Lord from heaven. The Bible tells us to trust in the Lord with all our heart, lean not unto our own understanding and in all our ways acknowledge the Lord and he shall direct our path. (29) Immediately after the tribulation of those days shall the sun be darkened, and the moon shall not give her light, and the stars shall fall from heaven, and the powers of the heavens shall be shaken: (30) And then shall appear the sign of the Son of man in heaven: and then shall all the tribes of the earth mourn, and they shall see the Son of man coming in the clouds of heaven with power and great glory.

Matt. (24:31-37): And he shall send his angels with a great sound of a trumpet, and they shall gather together his elect from the four winds, from one end of heaven to the other. In these verses of scriptures Jesus is describing his glorious return there will be no mistake when Jesus makes his return because the heavens will declare it, and he says that he will send his angels to gather all of the righteous, the ones that endured to the end. 32 Now learn a parable of the fig tree; When his branch is yet tender, and puttered forth leaves, ye know that summer is nigh: 33 So likewise ye when ye shall see all these things, know that it is near, even at the doors. 34 Verily I say unto you, this generation shall not pass, till all these things be fulfilled. 35 Heaven and earth shall pass away, but my words shall not pass away. Jesus teaching should create a spirit of watchfulness in all those that believe in him, if we can discern the season that we are in because of different events that takes place during that period we should be able to know by the signs that Jesus has given us to know that we need to be watchful, and always ready. The things that Jesus tells us to be aware of are already in the world, and becoming more and more intensive as the days are passing. Jesus declares that the only thing left standing would be his word, and then all will have to stand in judgment to give an account, the faithful will reap everlasting glory, and the wicked everlasting damnation where there shall be weeping and gnashing of teeth. 36 But of that day and hour knoweth no man, not the angels of heaven, but my father only.

Jesus is letting the world know that no one knows when he will return, not even the angels in heaven. How can we expect Jesus himself to give us the exact day of his return when he doesn't know himself? And why would God tell us, if God would tell us the day of Jesus return everyone in the world would wait until that very second to give their life to Christ. And that would defeat the purpose because it wouldn't be done out of love for him, but out of not wanting to be cast into hell. 37 But as the days of Noah were, so shall also the coming of the Son of man be.

Matt.(24:38-44): For as in the days that were before the flood they were eating and drinking, marrying and giving in marriage, until the day that Noah entered into the ark, (39) And knew not until the flood came, and took them all away, so shall also the coming of the Son of man be. (40) Then shall two be in the field; the one shall be taken, and the other left. (41) Two women shall be grinding at the mill; the one shall be taken, and one other left. (42) Watch therefore: for ye know not what hour your Lord doth come. (44) Therefore be ye also ready: for in such an hour as ye think not the Son of man cometh. In a time of indifference and carelessness the Lord lets us know that his coming will be during a time of unawareness, and suddenness just as it was during the time of Noah. The righteous will be aware of the sign and keep themselves ready just as Noah did, but the wicked and unbeliever's will not pay attention to the sign therefore they will be like the people during the time of Noah, one will be left and the other will be caught up to meet the Lord in the clouds. The Lord says that people will be going about their daily lives and then all of a sudden destruction comes upon us. 1 Thessalonians (5:3-6) For when they shall say, Peace and safety; then sudden destruction cometh upon them, as travail upon a woman with child; and they shall not escape. Paul compares the destruction that will come upon the world as a woman that is pregnant and at a point where there is no pain for a period of about nine months. Then some point within that ninth month sudden pain come that has never been experience. Sometimes the doctors try and pen point an exact date but that baby's coming when it's ready.

Just as the return of Jesus will be no man know for sure the day nor the hour. But ye, brethren, are not in darkness, that that day should overtake you as a thief. Ye are all the children of light, the children of the day: we are not of the night, nor of darkness. Therefore let us not sleep, as do others; but let us watch and be sober. Paul teaches us to be awake, alert, and prepared.

In this know that Jesus is shown returning in glory for his church. Look to the Lord's coming as a source of comfort and hope. Jesus coming is our hope in both life and death. Devote yourself wholeheartedly to the Lord so that you will be one in whom He finds faith when He comes. Let the hope of His coming strengthen and comfort you as you devote yourself to the Lord Jesus Christ. Be watchful get your house in order our redeemer draws nigh.

Seeking Those Things Above and Not Beneath

Matthew (6:19-21) Lay not up for yourselves treasures upon the earth, where moth and rust doth corrupt, and where thieves break through and steal. But lay up for yourselves treasures in heaven, where neither moth nor rust doth corrupt, and where thieves do not break through nor steal. For where your treasure is there will your heart be also. Jesus does not prohibit material possessions, or enjoying material things, but don't let your earthly things take presidents over the things of God. Matthew (6:33) reads: But seek ye first the kingdom of God, and his righteousness; and all these things shall be added unto you. Gods command is to seek him and his will first, and he says he will give you everything you need. So he's not concern about us having wealth just don't let your wealth become your God. The lord says that a kingdom divided cannot stand so if we try first to build up our earthly wealth and then try to squeeze God somewhere in between it want stand; because we have chosen to make him second when clearly the word says seek him first. In the world today people seem more concern with driving their nice cars, having the biggest house, throwing big parties to impress other. Working from sun up to sun down because they feel as if they have not earn enough money to live on; not realizing that when you are working that much you are working toward an early grave. Money should not control us we should control it. If we allow money to be the controlling facture in our life it will never be enough. Instead of working our live away we should look to the hills from which cometh our help all our help comes from the Lord.

We do have to work I am not saying not to, but don't make it your life's mission. The Bible says that a man that doesn't work doesn't eat. Life seems more like putting on a show, but we need to look deeper into living this one life that God has graciously giving us. God didn't give us this second chance to just think about me, myself and I. We were place in this earth to fellowship with God, to preserve it, to follow after his will. Jesus commissioned us to go into the world and preach the gospel to every creature. Our life is not about trying to have the best things in life it's about winning souls into the kingdom of God. To preach the gospel, (which is the good news) that Jesus Christ die for the sins of the world. If we shall confess our sins and acknowledge him as our Lord and Savior we shall be saved. From a life of eternal damnation to life everlasting, let me clarify something God want us to be blessed in everything, he wants his children to be wealth. Which mean nothing missing in our lives, nothing broken in our lives and for us not to be hurting from any area in our life. The Bible says that the wealth of the wicked is laid up for the just. It's just a matter of holding on; the wealth is about to transfer. Everything in this life is temporary and we can't take it with us when leave the world. That's why the Lord says to build on things that are eternal, on things that will last. The things that you treasure the most is the things you will seek after; if your mind is fixed on the world you will seek after the worldly things and if the things of God then seek the things of heaven where thieves can't break in and steal.

In this world we work so hard to build a comfortable life for us and our children. To give and provide for them things that they have need of plus things that they desire, and that is no different then what our heavenly father wants for us. The only requirement is to put him and his will first, not your job, not your spouse, not you children, family nor your friends. We work hard for the thing that we have just for thieves to break in and steal in a matter of minutes, and just that fast our peace is gone. If the treasure of our heart was set on the kingdom more than the world we wouldn't worry so much about things being taken. We should rejoice more because we didn't lose our lives, things can be replaced but once a life is taken there is nothing we can do about it accept pray that the treasure of their heart belonged to Christ Jesus. When we look at some of our brothers and sisters that have giving their lives to the Lord, we have a lot of us making statements saying that we would never compromise our Lord and Savior. But as soon as we make it big or what we call wealth we forget how we got there. And the Lord starts to become second in our lives. We record gospel music, we make movies about him where we can say his name without compromise. We have T.V. broadcasting show where we are allowed to speak freely about Jesus. Some believer's have become so wealth due to making Christian films and gospel music. But yet it doesn't seem as though it's enough for us. Now we have to do worldly movies with all kind of violent and act's of lust in them. Why do we always have to conform to the things of the world and yet they don't conform to the things of God?

When Jesus commissioned us to preach the gospel he didn't tell us to comprise him nor his word. He said if I be lifted up from the earth I'll draw all man unto me. When we tell non-believer' about Jesus or give testimony about where we were. It should be done to glorify out heavenly father. We should tell them how messed up our lives were until we gave our life to Jesus. We should let the world see the glory of God in us. Tell them how we feel when we look at all that the Lord has done for us. We go through our trials and tribulations but we done stay in them now, because we have a Savior that understands how we feel and we know that if we just hold to him he will make it alright. Jesus said for us to lift up his name by spreading the good news of him. So when we tell others about him, when we praise and give his name glory, when we give testimony we are lifting up his name. And the power of his name will do the drawing we don't have to conform to the things of the world to win people to Christ. Jesus representation speaks for itself we just need to learn how to approach people with love and kindness. If we continue to seek God first his word says that he will supply all our need, Philippians (4:19) reads: But my God shall supply all your need according to his riches in glory by Christ Jesus. We don't need to worry about our need being met because if we take care of God work he will take care of us. Our treasure should be the will of God, the Bible says where your heart is there will your treasure be also.

1John (2:15-16) Love not the world, neither the things that are in the world. If any man, love the world the love of the father is not in him. We can't love the things of the world more than we love God, if so his love is not in us. Why would we love things that we can easily lose? When we know that the love of the father toward us is the only thing that will last forever. That should be an easy choice to make. For all that is in the world, the lust of the flesh, and the lust of the eyes, and the pride of life, is not of the father, but is of the world. We need to understand that everything that the world offers: the lust of the flesh, the lust of the eyes, and the pride of life, are the basic for all sin. We should not love the world or what it offers more than we love God.

✎ *The things that God gives us or eternal*

The things in the world or only temporary; do not believe the lies that the world has much more to offer then God, everything belongs to the Lord. If our heart is not right then we are not rooted and grounded in the Lord. And we will have no self control, we will fall into the lust of having wealth and we will forget about God and will think that we got here all by ourselves. And then our treasure becomes the wealth of the world therefore turning our heart away from our first love which is the Lord Jesus Christ. 1Timothy (6:10-12): For the love of money is the root of all evil: which while some coveted after, they have erred from the faith, and pierced themselves through with many sorrows. There's nothing wrong will having money, money is not evil but the love of money is. When one has a love for money, money will rule that person instead of that person ruling it. Most people that love money more than anything else in life has a destructive life and will never do anything to help others and eventually their money will destroy them. It's so many people in the world that have a real need. Some are homeless eating out of trash cans there are people that are unable to take a bath because they have no home. And when they come around us we want to turn the other way instead of reaching out a helping hand. Some are on drugs, some are alcoholic, and some have been abused. But yet they turn to other to ask them to help when they are barely able to take care of their own needs. People are spending millions and millions of dollars on materialistic things. True it is theirs and they can do what they want with it, but have compassion on other. You cannot take it with you when you die, and you want spend it all before you leave this world. So why not help other, the Bible says that it is better to give then to receive. Matthew (16: 26) reads: For what is a man profited, if he shall gain the whole world, and lose his own soul? Or what shall a man give in exchange for his soul?

We should be willing to forsake all and take up our cross and follow Jesus to save our soul. That should not be a hard choice to make your money cannot buy your way into heaven or in any part of Gods kingdom. 1Timothy (6:11-12) But thou, O man of God, flee these thing; and follow after righteousness, godliness, faith, love, patience, meekness. Fight the good fight, lay hold on eternal life, whereunto thou art also called, and hast professed a good profession before many witnesses. Loving money opens our lives to the ultimate deception because the heart of the issue is Lordship a person cannot serve two masters at the same time meaning you cannot serve both God and money. We should pursue true riches, which are spiritual in nature: righteousness, godliness, faith, love, patience, and gentleness. Money has made a lot of people that thought they would never comprise Jesus, did just that: such as Judas betraying Jesus, Delilah betrayed Samson, and Ananias and Sapphira lied to the Holy Spirit because of money. Ask yourself a question do you really want to seek after thing on the earth rather than seeking heavenly things? James (1:17) Every good gift and every perfect gift is from above, and comes down from the father of lights, with whom there is no variation or shadow of turning. God is the source of all good, he is unchangeable, and he always keeps his promises. Colossians (3:1-4): If ye then be risen with Christ, seek those things which are above, where Christ sitteth on the right of God. Through Jesus we have been made righteous and complete, therefore we should seek the thing that are important to God. Our salvation has already been secured, so why would we want to throw it away by seeking after temporary things that will soon vanish away. The Lord says that the earth will pass away but his word will last forever. Understand that when Jesus died, our sinful nature died too. Our live is now hidden with Christ in God, so seek after things above and not beneath. (2) Set your affection on things above, not on things on the earth.

(3) For ye are dead, and your life is hid with Christ in God. (4) When Christ, who is our life, shall appear, then shall ye also appear with him in glory? That's why we seek things above they are eternal, earthly things fade. Don't let money change who you are and whom you stand for. Don't feel like we have to do it the way the world does it to win people to Christ. People think that Christian people don't have fun, and that their lives are boring. And that is far from the truth,

everything that God ask us to give up is for our own good because he loves us. Drinking alcohol causes liver disease, and can also causes you to get behind the wheel of a car and either kill yourself or someone else, because your ability becomes impaired, Smoking causes cancer, heart problems and other complications. As for having a good time with your spouse God created marriage; for you to enjoy each other. God is not the author of adultery just think how wonderful life could be without being convicted in your mind but having peace; because you are doing right by your mate. Not to mention the fact that you put your spouse at risk of diseases and also there are chances of having unwanted children. And there is also the risk of your life been taking by their spouse or even your own when it's brought into the light. We don't need drugs to get high all we need is the Holy Spirit. That is the best high that you will every experience there's nothing in the world like him. And the only side effect is that once you try him you will never get enough. Don't compromise Jesus when making movies and gospel music. If your movies are successful the way they are in a positive way, don't conform to making movies or music the way the world does, we have enough movies showing acts of violent. It's not all ways about making money it should be about lifting up the name of our Lord. Showing the love of him in us, showing that there are people in the world that are willing to live a godly life.

We all ways look at what people call the glamour life and wish we had half of what the people in Hollywood have. We don't look at the consequence, or behind the scene of having all that money but still feeling like something is missing. Most rich people that have not giving their lives to Jesus don't have self control when it comes to money they are heading down a pathway of destruction. Just look at our news stations they are always broadcasting where someone in the limelight has overdosed on drugs, in rehab for alcohol abuse. How people or bringing false allegations against them just to try and get money from them. They have fans that have tried to kill them because they are obsessed with them. Spending all that money changing their faces and body parts altering what God has giving them. When the Bible clearly says that God created us in his own image, these things doesn't just happen in Hollywood they are happening everywhere. But when you are covered by Jesus and have that confidence in him we know everything will be alright. Romans (8:28) read: And we know that all things work together for good to them that love God, to them who are the called according to his purpose. You can have all the money in the world, but without Jesus you will never be fulfilled. There is a spot in our heart that's reserved only for Jesus, he is the one that makes us complete in every way. The world's way has conditions, but the only condition God has is to accept his son Jesus Christ, to put him and his will first; and to allow him to love and to take care of us. Everything that the world offers God offers more and there's a promise attached everlasting life. We need to be seeking those things above and not beneath don't wait until it's too late receive him as your personal Lord and Savior.

Turning Back To Our First Love.

The book of Revelation chapter (2) the Lord is speaking to the church of Ephesus concerning their works, and their labor, and their patience and how they cannot bear those which do evil. Jesus was commending the church for what they had done and also that they had not fainted. But he told them that he have something against them. Revelation (2:4) reads: Nevertheless I have somewhat against thee, because thou hast left thy first love. Church we have left our first love which is Jesus Christ. We need to repent and turn away from the world and turn back to Jesus. We can't continue to have a foot in Jesus and a foot in the world. Revelation (3:15-16) reads: I know thy works, that thou art neither cold nor hot: I would thou wert cold or hot. So then because thou art lukewarm, and neither cold nor hot, I will spue thee out of my mouth. The Lord is telling the church to turn back to Jesus; to make up our mind on whom to serve. Jesus is saying if you are going to be for me then be for me, but if for the world then be for the world at least this way he knows who you are standing with. If you can't make a decision and you are trying to please him and the world he with have no part in you. The book of James says that a double minded man is unstable in all his ways. And if you are unstable in your ways you will find it hard to make sound decisions. You will never be able to stand on the word of God; neither will you have faith or patience in his word. It is an impossible task to do the commission of Jesus which is to go into all the world and minister the gospel to every creature.

If you are waving in your decision it will not work. Matthew (6:24) reads: No man can serve two masters: for either he will hate the one, and love the other; or else he will hold to the one, and despise the other. Ye cannot serve God and mammon. When Jesus walked among the people he always declared that he was doing the will of his father the one who since him. So, just as Jesus did the will of God the father so must we do the will of Jesus; Jesus was our example to follow. We must stop compromising our first love and turn back to him. Not just when all hell is busting loose in our lives but also when everything is going great. Everyone always finds it easy to say they are standing with the Lord when everything is going right. But the true faith is when you can stand when everything is going wrong. It's so easy to say I'm standing with him when we think we have everything under control, but yet we turn our back on him. But in times of trouble we run to Jesus for him to fix our lives. But then when he does we feel as if we don't need him anymore as if we have fixed it ourselves. The Lord needs the church to be on one accord, and not to be fighting among our other brothers and sisters in Christ Jesus. How can we be a witness if we have left our first love? How can we minister to non believers if they can't see us walking in the love of God for one another?

The world will know us by the fruit that we produce, Matthew (7:17-20) reads: Even so every good tree bringeth forth good fruit; but a corrupt tree bringeth forth evil fruit. A good tree cannot bring forth evil fruit; neither can a corrupt tree bring forth good fruit. Every tree that bringeth not forth good fruit is hewn down, and cast into the fire. Wherefore by their fruits ye shall know them. Therefore children of God we must walk accordingly to who we proclaim to be. So it's time to stop pretending to be Christians, turn back to our first love and show the world who we represent we need to lead by our life-style because that is what we are being judged by in the eyes of the world. God looks at our heart so therefore it does no good to try and hide things from the world man has no heaven or hell to put us in. God says that everything done in the dark he will bring to the light.

So if we know that God will eventually expose all our dark secrets why do we try and hide who we really are, or whom we are really serving. The Bible says choose ye this day whom ye will serve as for me and my house we will serve the Lord. We can fool ourselves, we can fool the world, but we cannot fool the Lord. And he will not allow us to fool the world any longer while saying we are servants of his. God says if we belong to him be separate from the world. God says that we are in the world but not of the world, we are being renewed in the spirit of our mind to be just as Jesus is. The Bible tells us Just as Jesus is so are we in this world. Jesus never forgot his first love, but we have and it shows by the way we live. Because we have put any and everything before him we fit him into our busy lives when it's on our mind to do so. Not realizing that's who we should thank for watching over us all night long, or for waking us up every morning clothed in our right mind. Jesus didn't have to do anything for us, but he did because he first loved us. We are not responsible for getting the jobs we have or for the car we drive, the roof over our head, breath in our bodies, clothes on our backs. Some of us maybe in pain but yet we are still here, because God kept us and he is still making a way, God is still on the throne, he still sits high and he looks low.

God saved us through grace we didn't save ourselves. It was a gift from God his son Jesus (the anointed one and his anointing) grace is unmerited favor. 2Corinthians (12: 9) reads: And he said unto me, my grace is sufficient for thee: for my strength is made perfect in weakness. Even when we are at our weakest the Lord has made himself available for us to lean and depend on him. In all that we go through mentally, physically, spiritually, and financially, he says to cast all our cared upon him for he cares for us. We just need to have our heart set back to our first love. Because in God, we breath, move, and have our being, and we know that in him according to Romans (8:28) reads: And we know that all things work together for good to them that love God, to them who are the called according to his purpose. Everything works for those that love God and if we are putting him and his will first in our lives we don't need to worry are be stressful about anything. Because God has it all worked out for our good we just need to keep our faith in him. We can't change anything by worrying the only thing worrying does is attack our health, our mind, our peace and our joy. The Bible says that the joy of the Lord is our strength. Don't allow the devil to steal your joy. Because in doing that he can disrupted your life, and he will eventually destroy you. John (10:10) reads: The thief cometh not, but for to steal, and to kill, and to destroy: I am come that they might have life, and that they might have it more abundantly. God has not turned his back on us so why should we turn away from him.

Psalms (23:1-6) reads; The Lord is my shepherd; I shall not want. He maketh me to lie down in green pastures: he leadeth me beside the still waters. He restoreth my soul: he leadeth me in the path of righteousness for his name's sake. Yea, though I walk through the valley of the shadow of death, I will fear no evil: for thou art with me; thy rod and thy staff they comfort me. Thou preparest a table before me in the presence of mine enemies: thou anointest my head with oil; my cup runneth over. Surely goodness and mercy shall follow me all the days of my life: and I will dwell in the house of the Lord forever. With Jesus why worry or be in distress he is our shepherd and a shepherd provide for and protect his sheep. And in this case our shepherd laid down his life for us.

✍ *Turn to Jesus before it's too late*

He make a way out of no way, things are impossible for man, but with the Lord nothing is impossible. Church we should not be turning away from our first love we should be praising his name and lifting up holy hands. Psalms (22:22) reads: I will declare thy name unto my brethren: in the midst of the congregation will I praise thee. The Lord is asking us the church to turn back to him: Revelation (2:5) Remember therefore from whence thou art fallen, and repent, and do the first works; or else I will come unto thee quickly, and will remove thy candlestick (church) out of his place, except thou repent. It does no good to repent if we are not going in the direction of Jesus. If we have repented and have not turned away from the world but are still moving in that direction then our repentance is in vain. True repentance means to turn around from the worldly ways and turn to Jesus and move in the direction of heaven.

As the Apostle Paul says: Brethren, I count not myself to have apprehended: but this one thing I do, forgetting those things which are behind, and reaching forth unto those things which are before, I press toward the mark for the prize of the high calling of God in Christ Jesus. We the church will know we love the Lord our God with all our heart when we seek him with all our heart. The church need to search for the Lord with all our heart, and when we do he says he will be found of us: Jeremiah (29: 12-14) reads: Then shall ye call upon me, and ye shall go and pray unto me, and I will hearken unto you. And ye shall seek me, and find me, when ye shall search for me with all your heart. And I will be found of you, saith the Lord: The Lord knows what in our heart and he also knows which ones are his. The ones that belong to him are still continuing toward heaven and not looking back because our focus is upon him. Because we know that all our help comes from the Lord, who is the author and finisher of our faith. People of God he whom has started a good work in us will not stop until we are complete. Jesus says if we endure to the end he will give us a crown of glory. Revelation (2:7) reads: He that hath an ear let him hear what the spirit saith unto the churches: To him will I give to eat of the tree of life, which is in the midst of the paradise of God.

The Lord is calling his church into a deeper level in him, but we must separate ourselves from the world. We must abide in him and let him abide in us. We must stop wavering in the things of God and turn back to our first love before it is too late. Everything that's happening in the world today should serve as a wakeup call for us to get our house in order. And to do what Jesus has commissioned us to do which is to preach the Gospel (the good news). Letting the world know that Jesus is the way, the truth, and the life and no one can get to the father but by him. The devil has his people representing, and they seem to be doing a good job of deceiving people into believing that there is no God the Father, God the Son, or God the Holy Spirit. Also that there is no Heaven or Hell and even if there is that no loving God would send his children to hell. But they are not realizing that God is the creator of all things but all are not his.

If we have not accepted his free gift which is his son the Lord Jesus Christ, God doesn't send us to hell we send ourselves by not accepting Jesus. The people that serve Satan has also blinded people into thinking that they have all the time in the world to make a decision on who to believe. Mean while time is running out, if we were to look back in the old testament of Bible, which is the spoken word of God. We will see that the history of it served as an example for us.

And the end resorts of the action that was taken when people did not heed the commandments of the Lord. God himself repented that he has made man; and now we are at a period in time where the world is in that same err of man turning away from God. And now we are running after all kinds of idols gods and the evil that's in man heart. We are so fixated on the lust and evilness that in the world until we can't see the truth. And we want see the truth until we make Jesus Lord of our live. Only then will we come out of the dark into the light and be set free. John (8:31-32) reads: Then said Jesus to the Jews which believed on him: If ye continue in my word, then are ye my disciples indeed: And ye shall know the truth, and the truth shall make you free. Church don't wait too long to turn back to Jesus our first love. And to those that have not accepted Jesus make your decision today. Don't listen to the devil his fate has already been decided. He will be cast into the lake of fire and brimstone where he will burn for all eternity. His mission is to take as many with him that's willing to be deceived. 2Chronicles (7:14) reads: If my people, which are called by my name, shall humble themselves, and pray, and seek my face, and turn from their wicked ways; then will I hear from heaven, and will forgive their sin, and will heal their land. God give us a choice in this scripture we don't have to put up with the world being the way it is today. God says if his people would turn from their wicked ways and pray he will fix everything. Some of us are too busy fighting each other, there is strength in the unity of prayer. If the body will stand together it will be strong and can withstand anything. If one part is weak then the whole body suffers together. If we learn how to strengthen our brother when he falls we can remain strong. How bad church, do we want to see God move on behalf of us, how bad do we want change? Look to our Lord and Savior Jesus Christ the same yesterday, today and forever.

It's Time to Stop Straddling the Fence .

Have you ever seen someone walking in two different directions at the same time? That's how life is if we are walking with Jesus and walking with the world; we are heading in two different directions one is heaven bound and the other is hell bound. Joshua (24:15) reads: Choose ye this day who you will serve, as for me and my house we will serve the Lord. It's time to stop straddling the fence, Matthew (6:24) reads: No man can serve two masters: for either he will hate one and love the other; or else he will hold to the one, and despise the other. Ye cannot serve God and mammon. In order for us to serve the Lord whole heartily we must let go of the things of the world, there should be nothing or no one put before God. Matthew (16:24-27) reads: Then said Jesus unto his disciples, if any man will come after me, let him deny himself, and take up his cross and follow me. For whosoever will save his life shall lose it: and whosoever will lose his life for my name sake shall find it. For what is a man profited, if he shall gain the whole world, and lose his own soul? Or what shall a man give in exchange for his soul? For the Son of man shall come in the glory of his father with his angels; and then he shall reward every man according to his works. When we make a conscience decision to follow Jesus, he says that we must first deny ourselves. That simply means we must put the kingdom of God above all because we cannot be effective to him unless we put him first. God put us first when he offered us his best and only which is his son Jesus Christ. So, why should he not expect us to give everything we are toward living for him?

❧ *We have the Spirit of God.*

Why should we have to give apart of ourselves to him and a part to the world? When he gave his all so through him we could be set free. All these things that we don't want to let go of, we can still have them and have them more abundantly with the Lord. Anything that the Lord gives doesn't fade away like the things of the world. So I say to us it's time to stop straddling the fence and make a choice and make sure it's a choice that we can live with. Because it could be the choice between heaven and hell, don't get caught somewhere in the middle if so our choice will be made for us and we might not like the outcome. We will never make conscience decisions by trying to have a kingdom mind set and a worldly mind set. A kingdom mindset is of a spiritual nature and the worldly mind set is of the flesh. The Bible says that the flesh cannot please God nor does it understand the things of God. God is a spirit and those that worship him must worship him in spirit and in truth. The flesh when it comes to understanding the things of God is spiritually discerned. 1Corinthians (2:9-14) reads: But as it is written, Eyes hath not seen, nor ear heard, neither have entered into the heart of man, the things which God hath prepared for them that love him. But God hath revealed them unto us by his spirit: for the spirit searcheth all things, yea, the deep things of God. For what man knoweth the things of a man, save the spirit of man which is in him? Even so the things of a God knoweth no man, but the spirit of God. Now we have received, not the spirit of the world, but the spirit which is of God; that we might know the things that are freely given to us of God.

Which things also we speak, not in the words which man's wisdom teacheth, but which the Holy Ghost teacheth; comparing spiritual things with spiritual. But the natural man receiveth not the things of the spirit of God: for they are foolishness unto him: neither can he know them, because they are spiritually discerned. In viewing these scriptures we learn that a person own inner thoughts are only know to himself. So the mind of God is known only by God's spirit God has chosen to make himself known in Jesus Christ, and the Holy Spirit has brought this revelation of Christ to the church through the apostles. Spirit answers to spirit, not spirit to mind, the Holy Spirit interprets spiritual things to spiritual people. So, therefore if you are straddling the fence how then can the carnal mind accepted the things of the spirit when the spirit can't reveal things to the flesh because the flesh is worldly? The spiritual man possessing spiritual maturity and has a nature for the truth, the natural man finds it difficult to understand him, and he lives more for human opinion than for Christ. 1Corinthians (14:33) reads: For God is not the author of confusion, but of peace, as in all the churches of the saints. There is no peace within us if we are straddling the fence because we are warring within ourselves. Trying to make a decision on which direction to follow, when all we need to do is turn it over to Jesus and rest in his peace. We must make the commit to God if we are going to serve him and turn from the world because we cannot serve both.

1Corinthians (10:21) reads: Ye cannot drink the cup of the Lord, and the cup of devils: ye cannot be partakers of the Lords table and of the table of devils. Do we provoke the Lord to jealousy? Are we stronger than he? We cannot sit at both tables at the same time; neither can we walk in two different directions at the same time. It is an impossible task and God is the only author of doing the impossible. We can only come to God in spirit the Bible tells us that those that worship God must worship him in spirit and in truth. So it is impossible for us to connect to God with our foot wrap in the world, God cannot communicate with the flesh. So why are we still straddling the fence? Why is it so hard for us to let the world go? The Lord says we are in the world but not of the world, he says come from among them be ye separated. We live in the world but our mind set doesn't have to be of the world. When we are in Jesus we have a kingdom mind set, therefore we should be walking in the same direction. James (1:8) reads: A double-minded man is unstable in all his ways. A double-minded man is a person drawn in two opposite direction. His allegiance is divided and because of his lack of sincerity it can alter his prayer life and his faith in God. Because the flesh doesn't believe in God, therefore there will always be a fight for control.

We cannot completely give ourselves to Jesus whole heartily until we make up our mind to stop straddling the fence. We may not be melting down gold to make Idol gods. But we do have things that we idolize which are our jobs, houses, cars, clothes, money, our spouse, our children and even our parents. The Lord says that if we are to follow him we must forsake all. Not to have a foot in him and a foot in the world. But to pick up our cross and follow him not just when things are going wrong, but also when everything seem to be going good. Don't just praise him on Sunday's and Monday-Saturday we don't acknowledge him. Don't just call on him in times of trouble, or when we are broke, disgusted, and can't be trusted by the world. People in the world will always have a condition to love you, when the only condition Jesus has is to accept him and put him first so he can love us. Everything that the world offers God offers also and more Ephesians (3: 19-20) reads: Now unto him that is able to do exceeding abundantly above all that we ask or think, according to the power that worketh in us.

God can do above what our mind is not able to handle, or understand. Isaiah (55:8-9): For my thoughts are not your thoughts, neither are your ways my ways, saith the Lord. For as the heavens are higher than the earth, so are my ways higher than your ways, and my thoughts than your thoughts. Jeremiah (29:11): For I know the thoughts that I think toward you, saith the Lord, thoughts of peace, and not of evil, to give you an expected end. The world and the things of the world are only a temporary fix. But for some reason we still want to keep one foot in the world and one foot in the kingdom, or we testing God to see how long he will allow us to straddle the fence? 1John (4:4) tells us that greater is he that is in us than he that is in the world. We will never get the revelation of the true power that is in us if we don't allow the Spirit of God to help us turn completely away from the world and turn to Jesus. That's what he's here for, the Holy Spirit is our enable to help us in our weakness.

Romans (8:26-28): likewise the Spirit also helpeth our infirmities: for we know not what we should pray for as we ought: but the Spirit itself maketh intercession for us with groaning which we cannot be uttered. And he that searcheth the hearts knoweth what is the mind of the Spirit, because he maketh intercession for the saints according to the will of God. So if our prayer is to turn away for the world and to put our whole heart into serving Jesus, and we know that is the will of God for our lives, then if we ask him the Holy Spirit will enable us to do it, but he cannot help us if we have not made a conscience decision to stop straddling the fence. Verse 28 reads: And we know that all things work together for good to them that love God, to them who are the called according to his purpose. Somehow we have chosen to entertain the thought that the devil has put into our mind that if we give ourselves total over to Jesus that we will lose all control of who we feel we are and the rights that we think we have, that we will no longer have any say so of what we want to do, and that is our flesh speaking it does not want to give ownership over to Jesus, and that's why we are still straddling the fence.

When we accepted Jesus as Lord and Savior of our lives, we repented and asked for forgiveness of our sins, repent means to turn from the life we were living and begin this new life with Jesus to be not conformed to the world but be transformed by the renewing of our mind, to take off corruption and to put on that which is incorruptible, to stop thinking as the world thinks but to think as Jesus thinks; have you heard the people say (what would Jesus do) think about it. The bible tells us to let this mind be in you which was also in Christ Jesus. 1 Corinthians 3:16-17 reads: Know ye not that you are the temple of God, and that the Spirit of God dwelleth in you? If any man defile the temple of God, him shall God destroy; for the temple of God is holy, which temple ye are. We cannot mix the Spirit of God with the spirit of the world and that's what we continue to do when we choose to continue to straddle the fence.

✍ *The flesh cannot understand the things of God.*

2Corinthians 6: 14-17 reads: Be ye not unequally yoked together with unbelievers: for what fellowship hath righteousness with unrighteousness? And what communion hath light with darkness? And what concord hath Christ with Belial (wicked)? Or what part hath he that believeth with an infidel (unbeliever)? And what agreement hath the temple of God with idols? For ye are the temple of the living God; as God hath said, I will dwell in them, and walk in them; and I will be their God, and they shall be my people. Wherefore come out from among them, and be ye separate, saith the Lord, and touch not the unclean thing; and I will receive you. God received us when we accepted his son Jesus, so therefore we are clean through the washing of the blood of Jesus. So why do we keep choosing to hold on to that which the Lord says is unclean? Where God says be not unequally yoked, we assume that he is merely speaking on whether a person is going to church or not. But as Christians we must look a little deeper, we must look on the inside of the persons heart. The Lord is saying do not hook his spirit up with the spirit of the world, because his spirit and the spirit of the world have nothing in common. One is of a good nature and the other is of a defile nature. It's as if putting gas and fire together sooner or later there will be an explosion. James (4:4) reads: Adulterers and adulteresses! Do you not know that friendship with the world is enmity with God? Whoever therefore wants to be a friend of the world makes himself an enemy with God. That is a clear case of breaking our vows to love and to serve God, when we are straddling the fence?

In marriage we take a vows to love, honor, and obey till death do us part. Then one of them starts a relationship with someone other than their spouse it causes all kinds of confusion. It takes away your peace, your time, and your health starts to fell because of stress from trying to live two different lives. Trying to be in two different places at the same time and trying to please two different people while trying not to be exposed. It will soon become an impossible task to maintain, and we will have to make a choice of who is more important. Our plan to keep serving the Lord and the world will eventually lead to destruction. It is impossible to have a foot that reaches the gateway to heaven and the gateway to hell; it's time to have both feet going in the same direction. If you choose to serve Jesus then serve him but if the world then serve the world. Just make sure you choose before it is too late, don't let a choice be made for you. If you are straddling the fence that could mean you doesn't have enough faith in Jesus to supply all of our need. In the book of Revelation Jesus says that he has one thing against us and that is we have left our first love, because we have chosen not to put him first in our lives.

This world is not our home it is just a temporary place for us, but in Jesus there is eternal life, and in the world there is destruction at every turn. The Lord said that he would rather for us to be either hot or cold because if we are lukewarm he will spue us out of his mouth, we will lose the intimacy that we have with Jesus. what we must realize is that the world and the things of the world robs us of our time serving the Lord and following after righteousness, we can still have everything that the world offers and have it more abundantly with Jesus, the things in the world are temporary but the things of God are eternal. The bible says that the Lord will give us the desires of our heart: But we must seek first the kingdom of God and his righteousness and all these things shall be added unto you Matthew 6:33. Hebrews 12:1-2 reads: Lay aside everything that we allow to draw our attention away from being able to serve the Lord with a pure heart, and everything that compromise our relationship with serving him to the fullest.

We cannot give our all to Jesus when we are still chasing behind the world. Galatians 5:1 reads: Stand fast therefore in the liberty wherewith Christ hath made us free; be not entangled again with the yoke of bondage, when we are straddling the fence we are trying to mix freedom with bondage, Christ set us free and we still act as if we can't let go of being bound, still dragging those chains everywhere we go, the Bible says that whom the Son sets free is free indeed. Abraham had a child with a bondwoman who was born after the flesh, and he also had a child with a freewoman which was by promise, but in order for him to receive the child which was by promise he had to release the child of the bondwoman from his household, in order for us to be effective to our Lord and Savior Jesus Christ we must release the bondage which is the flesh because it want mix with the Spirit of freedom. When will we make the choice to stop having an affair on Jesus with the world, and put both feet in his direction. It's Time to stop straddling the fence.

What the World Needs Now Is A Miracle.

The world as we know it today has taken a turn for the worst. People are not looking at the changes that are happening, because we tell ourselves that this have been happening since our parent and our grandparents were young. Not taking into consideration that things are escalating. Violent on almost every streets corner, there are times that I can remember when people fought one other with their words or with their fist now, it's with guns and knives. Some of our children are selling drugs, and more importantly their selling them to other children in their own neighborhood. Killing one other over nothing, carjacking people at gun point, breaking into people homes without a thought that they could lose their lives as well as take someone else life. Our young people are suppose to be the future of the world, but the way they are going is down that wide road that leads to destruction. Joel (2:28) reads: And it shall come to pass afterward, that I will pour out my spirit upon all flesh; and your sons and your daughters shall prophesy, your old men shall dream dreams, your young men shall see visions. God has a plan for our young people, but how will they know if we don't tell them who God is and the plans that he has for their lives. What the world needs now is a miracle. Matthew (7:13-14) reads: Enter ye in at the strait gate: for wide is the gate, and broad is the way, that leaded to destruction and many there be which go in thereat. Because strait is the gate, and narrow is the way, which leadeth unto life, and few there be that find it.

That wide gate is people going through life without Jesus, and without Jesus we will never see that the life we are living is not the right way. We will never understand that the things that we are doing is because of the darkness that is within our heart. Right now we are in that dark place, we feel as if we are justified in the things that we do and the way we live. And that is because we are still guided by the nature world. The Bible tells us that the devil is the prince of this world. But there is another away out, we just can't see it now because the devil has blinded us and shielded us from the truth. The only way anyone can be set free from that bondage mentality is when we accept Jesus. When we live our lives this way we are living just as Satan wants us to live. Satan is on a mission to destroy, John (10:10-11) reads: The devil cometh not but for to steal, and to kill, and to destroy: I am come that they might have life, and that thy might have it more abundantly. Jesus says I am the good shepherd: the good shepherd giveth his life for the sheep. We have to make a choice we can either choose someone that wants to leads us down a path of destruction and death or someone that wants to leads us down a path of abundant and eternal life. Jesus laid down his life for us so we could be free. Satan is not trying to love, protect, or provide for us and he definitely did not give his life for us.

The only thing he will ever do is what he is doing right now and that is to get us to destroy one another. And we are so clueless to his devices. We allow ourselves to be used by him and will continue to do so without Jesus being Lord of our lives. At some point we need to realize that this way of living is wrong, there is only a temporary fix of peace, joy, love, compassion and they last but for a moment. There is only hatred in living life this way, because Jesus is the only one that can teach us what love is. Jesus showed unconditional love when he died on the cross for our sins. To restore what was given away by Adam and Eve. Jesus set us free so that we could have eternal life, so that we can have peace, love, and happiness. We don't have to wait until we get to heaven we can have it right now through him. What the world needs now is a miracle.

In order to get that life that we desire we must first turn everything that we are over to Jesus. Jesus is the potter and we are the clay, he is the author and the finisher of our faith if he said it that will he do it. The Lord says that he will never leave us nor forsake us, that he will be with us to the end of time. Romans (12: 1-2) reads: I beseech you therefore, brethren, by the mercies of God, that ye present you bodies a living sacrifice, holy, acceptable unto God, which is your reasonable service. And be not conformed to this world: but be ye transformed by the renewing of your mind, that ye may prove what is that good, and acceptable, and perfect, will of God. When our mind is renewed by the word of God the Bible tells us that we have the mind of Christ. When we walk in that mind set it come naturally for us to love and treat one another right. If we don't know how to love ourselves it will be impossible for us to love anyone else, and the Lord is the only one that can show us how to love. What the world needs now is a miracle. When was the last time we seen people show genuine love for one another. Or people helping each other without a motive, taking care of the elderly or praying for our young people. When was the last time we have tried to encourage our children and show them the right path; instead of talking down on them? Have we told them there is a better way which is Jesus? How hard can it be to go and tell the world that Jesus loves them and cares about them? That no matter what they have done Jesus can still work a miracle in their lives, all they have to do is turn their life over to him. And let them know that it will not cost them anything other than to say here I am Lord I give you my life.

We must also let them know that the journey will not be easy, but if they just trust in the all mighty God he will bring them through. That their life does not have to be about death, it can be about living life to the fullest. In Jesus we can see real miracles he has not stopped doing miracles because he ascended to heaven. Jesus performs a miracle in our lives every morning when he wakes us up. Jesus is still performing we just have to apply our faith in his word. Just like in the old testaments days of our Bible when the Lord open the mouth of a donkey. Numbers (22:28) reads: And the Lord opening the mouth of an ass, and she said unto Balaam, what have I done unto thee, that thou hast smitten me these three times? If the Lord can open the mouth of an ass, what is impossible for him to do in our live if we just seek him first? 2Kings chapter 5 tells about a man named Naaman who was captain of the host of the king of Syria. The Bible says that he was a great man with his master and honorable because by him the Lord had given deliverance unto Syria: he was also a mighty man in valour, but he was a leper, and God through one of his prophet, Elisha healed him of his leprosy. 2Kings (5:10) reads: And Elisha sent a messenger unto him, saying, go and wash in Jordan seven times, and thy flesh shall come again to thee, and thou shalt be clean, sometimes what God instructs us to do something it may not make sense to us, but in order to receive what he has for us we must be obedient. Naaman was wroth and went away because to him it made no sense, so therefore he did not get cleaned of his leprosy until he was obedient to God's word.

2Kings (5:14-15) reads: Then went he down, and dipped himself seven times in the Jordan, according to the saying of the man of God: and his flesh came again like unto the flesh of a little child, and he was clean. And he returned to the man of God, he and all his company, and came and stood before him: and he said, behold, now l know that there is no other God in all the earth. What the world needs now is a miracle? Mark (16:17-18) reads: And these signs shall follow them that believe; in my name shall they cast out devils; they shall speak with new tongues:

They shall take up serpents; and if they drink any deadly thing, it shall not hurt them: they shall lay hands on the sick, and they shall recover. What is Jesus saying here? That we are joint heirs with the miracle maker all we need to do is apply our faith mixed with his name. God can do all things but fail, and we can do all things through Christ who give us strength. John (15: 4, 5, 7,) reads: Abide in me, and I in you, as the branch cannot bear fruit of itself except it abide in the vine, ye are the branches: He that abideth in me, and I in him, the same bringeth forth much fruit: for without me ye can do nothing. If ye abide in me and my words abide in you ye shall ask what ye will, and it shall be done unto you. Without Jesus we can do nothing, but in him we can do all things. So why is the world being so control by the enemy? when God word says in 2 Chronicles (7:14) reads: If my people, which are called by my name, shall humble themselves, and pray, and seek my face, and turn from their wicked ways; then will I hear from heaven, and will forgive their sin, and will heal their land. That's the miracle the world need is for God's people the believers, to turn from our wicked ways. To come together in the unity if prayer and pray for the world, and allow God to do what he said he will do. God will heal our land. The miracle we need is in us through the word of God in the name of Jesus. When was the last time we laid hands on the sick, open the blind eyes, or open the deaf ear, or open the mouth of the mute, raise the dead, or preach the gospel to the world in the name of Jesus?

Have we not done these miracles because we have no faith in God's word? Or is it that we are waiting for other to move first just like we do when we are in church. We want give God praise, or lift up our hands to worship, or say hallelujah unless someone does it first, and then we follow suit. Someone did move first, the Lord Jesus Christ and now he's waiting for us to do what he commissioned us to do in his name. Don't be fearful of the world 2Timothy (1:7) reads: For God hath not given us the spirit of fear; but of power, and of love, and of a sound mind. In Jesus name there is power in us. 1John (4:4) reads: Ye are of God, little children, and have overcome them: because greater is he that is in you, than he that is in the world. God gave us the Holy Spirit which is power within us, so have you activated the power on the inside of you? Psalms (27:1) reads: The Lords is my light and my salvation; whom shall I fear? The Lord is the strength of my life; of whom shall I be afraid. We should not be afraid to use the power that is within us. Every time we lay hands on the sick, or give sight to the blind, open the deaf ear or the mute mouth, or when we preach the gospel in the name of Jesus it brings glory to God our heavenly father.

Matthew (5:13-16) reads: Ye are the salt of the earth: but if the salt has lost his savor, wherewith shall it be salted? It is thenceforth good for nothing, but to be cast out, and to be trodden under foot of men. Ye are the light of the world a city that is set on a hill cannot be hid. Neither do men light a candle, and put it under a bushel but on a candlestick; and giveth light unto all that are in the house. Let your light so shine before men, that they may see your good works, and glorify your father which is in heaven. We need to recognize that our life has either a positive or a negative effect. We should be living to do the will of God responsibly to bring glory to his name. When Jesus prayed and did miracles there was never a doubt in him. It was not about pride or self glory, Jesus said he came to do the will of his father.

✍ *Allow the Holy Spirit to lead you in all your ways.*

We should follow Paul's example, 1Corinthians (2: 4-5) reads: And my speech and my preaching was not with enticing words of man's wisdom, but in demonstrations of the spirit and of power. That your faith should not stand in the wisdom of men, but in the power of God. Know ye not that you are the temple of God, and that the spirit of God dwelleth in you? 1Corinthians (4:20) reads: For the kingdom of God is not in word, but in power. We are connected to the kingdom which is power it's not about us it's about the commission of Jesus. We have to stir up the power that is in us, and learning to use the authority that he has given us. Demons trembling at the name of Jesus, but we also need to have faith because these evil spirits can tell when we are unsure of our authority. They can tell when we are bold and confidence and when we are timid and wavering in our belief. If we are doubtful in our faith we are just like that candle that is suppose to let its light shine for all the world to see, but is still covered by darkness. John chapter (9) tells us that Jesus healed a man that was blind from his birth, and his disciples ask him saying, master, who did sin this man or his parents, that he was born blind? Jesus answered, neither hath this man sinned nor his parents: but that the works of God should be made manifest in him. I must work the works of him that sent me, while it is day: the night cometh, when no man can work. As long as I am in the world, I am the light of the world. Jesus was not talking about the light from the sunshine.

He was speaking about doing the will of our father while we still have breath in our body, while we still have our health, and able to get out among the world. To go forth while we still have strength in our body to be that light, going out into the world to perform miracles, signs, and wonders in his name. What the world needs now is for us to be that miracle through the name of Jesus. Mark 11: (22-24) reads: And Jesus answering saith unto them have faith in God. For verily I say you, that whosoever shall say unto this mountain, be thou removed, and be thou cast into the sea; and shall not doubt in his heart, but shall believe that those things which he saith shall come to pass: he shall have whatsoever he saith, therefore I say unto you, what things so ever ye desire, when ye pray, believe that ye receive them and ye shall have them. What do you believe? What the world needs now is a miracle.

Privileges We Have As Believers.

(Access to God: Romans (5:1-2)
Romans 5: 1-2 reads: Therefore being justified by faith, we have peace with God through our Lord Jesus Christ: By whom also we have access by grace wherein we stand, and rejoice in hope of the glory of God. Through the shed blood of Jesus we have been declared righteous, Jesus who was sinless, carried all our sins upon him, nailed them to the cross, buried them in the grave, and rose out of the grave the third day with all power. Because of Jesus we are declared righteous in the sight of God. When God look at us he's sees us through the shed blood of his son Jesus, who washed us with his precious blood of all unrighteousness. We were saved through the gift that God gave us and that is grace which is his son Jesus. Although we did nothing to deserve it Jesus loved us enough to take on himself a punishment that was not his own. All who believe in Jesus not only shares in his death and burial, but we also share in his resurrection, and the benefit of eternal life.

(Christ's intercession: Hebrews (7:25-26)
Wherefore he is able also to save them to the uttermost that comes unto God by him, seeing he ever liveth to make intercession for them. For such an high priest became us, who is holy, harmless, undefiled, separate from sinners, and made higher than the heavens. We have

Jesus who took off his glory that he had in heaven to be born in this sinful world. In a physical body to experience the things that we would go through while we are in this body. So that he could understand and have compassion on us, and to be able to intercede on our behalf. John (17:5) reads: And now, O Father, glorify thou me with thine own self with the glory which I had with thee before the world was. Jesus gave up a lot for us to have these privileges through him. And we should do all we can to live a holy and righteous life, to show him that this chance that he has given us is not in vain.

(Everlasting life: John (17: 2-3)
These words spake Jesus, and lifted up his eyes to heaven, and said, Father, the hour is come; glorify thy son, that thy son may also glorify thee. As thou hast given him power over all flesh, that he should give eternal life to as many as thou hast given him. Jesus petition was not selfish, his desire was to glorify he father, and to glorify himself was to make himself known. Jesus was to soon be manifested as the savior of the world thus believers through knowing Jesus will know the father and therefore have eternal life.

(Intercession of the Spirit: Romans (8:16-17)
The spirit itself beareth witness with our spirit, that we are the children of God: And if children, then joint-heirs; with Christ; if so be that we suffer with him, that we may be also glorified together. The Holy Spirit gives us assurance that we are the children of God, God therefore leads his children through suffering before we can reach his glory, we have to be changed from that old nature, the bible tells us that we must be transformed by the renewing of our mind, and we can be renewed without going through something, suffering bring about perfection.

(Kinship with Christ: Hebrews (2:10-14)
For it became him, for whom all things, and by whom are all things, in bringing many sons unto glory, to make the captain of their salvation perfect through suffering. For both he that sanctifieth and they who are sanctified are all of one: For which cause he is not

ashamed to call them brethren. Saying, I will declare thy name unto my brethren in the midst of the church will I sing praise unto thee. And again, I will put my trust in him. And again, Behold I and the children which God hath given me. Forasmuch then as the children are partakers of flesh and blood, he also likewise himself took part of the same; that through death he might destroy him that had the power of death, that is, the devil; The path that Jesus tread as the suffering redeemer was fitting, for thereby he was made perfect. This does not mean that Jesus had virtue shortcomings but that he became perfect and complete as an all sufficient savior. Only through the suffering of temptation and death did he qualify to be our captain. There is a profound unity between Jesus and the ones he saved, whereby we became brethren through his physical birth, which we shared through our descent from Adam, and because of the new birth we became member of Gods family.

(Membership in God's kingdom 1Corinthians (6:9-11)
But, beloved, we are persuaded better things of you, and things that accompany salvation, though we thus speak. For God is not unrighteous to forget your work and labor of love, which ye have shewed toward his name, in that ye have ministered to the saints, and do minister. And we desire that every one of you shew the same diligence to the full assurance of hope unto the end. As believers we are made righteous and holy through Jesus. We are called to live holy lives holy living requires that we rely fully on the Lord's wisdom. We are able to understand and to know the ways of God through the Holy Spirit. And the Holy Spirit enable us to live as God's people, holy and set apart from the world, thus bring us into the membership of God's kingdom.

(Name written in heaven: Revelation (20:15)
And whosoever was not found written in the book of life was cast into the lake of fire. Those of us that have accepted Jesus as our Lord and savior, and have been doing the will of God our father and endured to the end, we shall be found in the book of life. But those that have not accepted Jesus as Lord and savior and have not done the will of

God the father shall not be found, he shall say depart from me I never knew you.

(Partakers of the divine nature: 2Peter (1:4)
Whereby are given unto us exceeding and precious promises: that by these ye might be partakers of the divine nature, having escaped the corruption that is in the world through lust. With these gifts we can share in being like God and the world will not ruin us with its evil desires.

(Reconciled to God: Romans (5:10)
For if, when we enemies, we were reconciled to God by the death of his Son, much more, being reconciled, we shall be saved by his life. While we were Gods enemies, we became his friends through the death of his son. God proved his love by giving his son to die on our behalf. We as Christians now have peace with God because we have been forgiven. We can rejoice because we are assured of our salvation.

(Suffering with Christ: (Acts: 5:41)
And they departed from the presence of the council, rejoicing that they were counted worthy to suffer shame for his name. As it was for the Apostles to rejoice in the suffering with Christ, we also should feel honored to suffer with the Lord who took our place in death, to give us eternal life. Jesus did not promise that we wouldn't go through trials and tribulations, it was just the opposite, but he does promise us a joy that is inexpressible and full of glory. Jesus also tells us to be of good cheer because he has overcome the world.

(Trials overcome: 1Peter (1:6-8)
Wherein ye greatly rejoice, though now for a season, if need be, ye are in heaviness through manifold temptations. That the trails of your faith, being much more precious than of gold that perisheth, though it be tried with fire, might be found unto praise and honor and glory at the appearing of Jesus Christ: Whom having not seen, ye love; in whom, though now ye see him not, yet believing, ye rejoice with joy unspeakable and full of glory. Remember that as we endure suffering,

our faith is being refined as with fire and we should value our faith more then we value gold looking toward the coming of our Lord and Savior Jesus Christ; so that our faith has been tested will result in praise, honor, and glory to Jesus.

(Victorious living: Romans (8:37-39)
Nay, in all these things we are more than conquerors through him that loved us. For I am persuaded, that neither death, nor life, nor angels, nor principalities, nor powers, nor things present, nor things to come. Nor height, nor depth, nor any other creature, shall be able to separate us from the love of God, which is in Christ our Lord. Through all these things we have full victory through God who showed his love for us. God's love is not as a human would love, his love is not normal his sees our sins and yet he still loves us. And when we come to him, he doesn't turn us away. God is there whether we walk away from him or not. Thank God for his acceptance of us because it's based on the finished work of Jesus and not on our own merit. We should be persuaded that absolutely nothing can separate us from the love of God in Jesus. God has made us more than conquerors in all things through Jesus who loves us. This truth should lead us to worship and wholehearted devotion.

Food for thought: Through Christ's crucifixion, burial, and resurrection, we have been set free from slavery to sin and made alive and victorious in the Spirit. Our old sinful life was crucified and buried with Jesus. Therefore, we now have his power at work in us to resist wrong behavior. By grace and the power of the Holy Spirit, we are free to live our lives in holiness, give our lives daily as worship to God, and be transformed in our thinking.

To God be the glory to, God be the praise Amen.

What Is A Christian?

The first time the word Christians was presented, was when the disciples was called Christians in Antioch. Acts (11: 26): And when he had found him, he brought him unto Antioch: And it came to pass, that a whole year they assembled themselves with the church, and taught much people, and the disciples were called Christians first in Antioch. The word Christians means Christ-like. When we accept Jesus as our Lord and Savior, being a Christians doesn't stop there. If we have made Jesus Lord of our lives, we have to find out who he is, what he did, and what the commitment of his life is; which is to do the will of his father. We can't be a Christian until we accept Jesus. Then we get in the word of God so we can develop a relationship with Christ. In order to develop a relationship with someone we must spend some one on one time with that person. We can never learn people, because people are still changing, and still finding their identity. Where on the other hand Christ never changes, the Bible say that he is the same yesterday, today, and forever, and we have his DNA in written form. We don't have to take anyone's word for who he is, we have the witness of God the father, and God the Holy Spirit. When we become Christians we repent, repent means to turn away from our old lives. Away from our old way of thinking, and begin our new journey of learning who we are now. So we must go back to where it all began, the Book of Genesis.

The Bible has three sections, which are the beginning, the middle, and an end. Before Christ; during Christ, and after Christ, but in hind sight he is the beginning, the middle and the end. Revelation 1:8: I am Alpha and Omega, the beginning and the ending, saith the Lord, which is, and which was, and which is to come, the Almighty. The beginning tells of how God created the world, by his spoken words. How he created everything that one would have need of then he created man and gave man a help meet? God said that it was not good that man should alone; so he created a woman. When God created man he was not lonely, but this was someone that he could have fellowship with, someone that was created in their image. Genesis (1:1): In the beginning God created the heaven and the: Genesis (1:26): And God said, Let us make man in our image, after our likeness: and let them have dominion over the fish of the sea, and over the fowls of the air, and over the cattle, and over all the earth, and over every creeping thing that creepeth upon the earth. Everything that God made was perfect; it was his will be done, his kingdom come, on earth as it is in heaven. The only commandment that God gave to man, was out of everything that he had created it belong to them for enjoyment; but the tree of the knowledge of good and evil belongs to him. How many times has God told us that we can have anything that our heart desires, but there's one thing I require of you? That when he tells you not to touch that or not to go to certain places, just trust me I have it all planned out. And we don't listen and find ourselves in a mess, because we thought we knew better than the creator.

Why do we always want, what God says that we cannot have? The answer is easy because that is the flesh speaking. (Foot note) anytime you desire what someone else has or you desire something more than you desire God or the things of God, we are in the operation of the flesh. That is not Christ-like, there's nothing wrong with wanting to have nice things. God wants his children to have everything we desire, but not ahead of him and not someone else's. Being Christ-like is realizing what Jesus put first, and that was the will of his father.

✎ *Put on the whole armor of God.*

Jesus was obedient to what God told him to do. 1Samuel (15:22): And Samuel said, Hath the Lord as great delight in burnt offerings and sacrifices, as in obeying the voice of the Lord? Behold, to obey is better than sacrifice, and to hearken than the fat of rams. Why, because if we are obedient to God's word we will have no problem with sacrifice. Not only is being a Christian walking in obedience, but also walking in the love of God one toward another. It's easy to walk in love when we realize who we really are in Christ Jesus. We are created by the author of love which is God our heavenly father. We are created in the image of God, our true identity is a Spirit being, we possess a soul (mind), and we live in a body. We are made from the dust of the ground, but the spirit come from God, who breathed into mans nostrils the breath of life. When we look into the mirror we should see the spirit of God, if we see ourselves we have not spent enough time declaring our true identity. Somehow we must learn how to detach our true identity from this fleshy body that we live in. And the only way to do that is by feeding our soul, which is our mind; what the word of God says about who we are in Christ Jesus. The Bible tells us that old things have passed away, Behold all things have become new. But in order for the old things to stay away, we must continually feed our soul the things that we feed our spirit man so that our soul can line up with our spirit instead of with our flesh, and that would be the word of God.

Flesh builds strength from the things of the world, and the spirit build from the things of God. Just how we were raised in the things of the world, now, we must start over as new born babe and be raised in the word of God. Our flesh may have grown on the outside, but the inside is where we make the change from adulthood to an infant. When we start to change our way of thinking, we soon become more Christlike. We must feed on the word daily in order to walk accordingly in our identity as a Christian. We will not need to tell anyone that we are Christians, because once the inside starts to be renewed our walk we be transformed also. Meaning the way we treat others will change, people will be able to see that joy and peace that we have now. Because how we feel on the inside always shows up on the outside, not only that but there are things we use to do and places we use to go we will not have that desire anymore. We will be mindful of what we allow to come out of our mouth, therefore being slow to speak and quick to hear. We will allow the spirit to teach us how to love ourselves and other as Christ loves us. Ephesians (6:10-13) reads: Finally, my brethren, be strong in the Lord, and in the power of his might. Put on the whole armor of God that ye may be able to stand against the wiles (tricks) of the devil. For we wrestle not against flesh and blood, but against principalities, against powers, against the rulers of the darkness of this world, against spiritual wickedness in high places. Wherefore take unto you the whole armor of God that ye may be able to withstand in the evil day, and having done all, to stand.

As Christians we don't have to fight this battle against the devil, because the battle belongs to God, he told us when we have done all to stand just stand and see the salvation of the Lord. God has already won the battle; we have to control the battle of our thoughts with God's word. We now know that this battle is not our, it's the Lord, he told us to stand on his word, to have faith in him and to trust that his word will do what he says it will do. Isaiah 55:11: So shall my word be that goeth forth out of my mouth: it shall not return unto me void, but it shall accomplish that which I please, and it shall prosper in the thing whereto I sent it.

We have it all wrong we feel like we must fight the devil, when God clearly says in his word that we have authority in Jesus name. There is a battle we do have to fight which the Lord can't or will not fight for us. And that is the battle of our spirit man and our carnal man, that battle belongs to us. Galatians (5:17): For the flesh lusteth against the Spirit, and the Spirit against flesh: and these are contrary the one to the other: so that ye cannot do the things that ye would. But God did give us instructions to win that battle if we choose to follow his directions: We must follow God's word just as it is written, if we leave out or change one word it become in effective. In order for us to be Christ-like we need to always keep our eyes on Jesus. Just as Apostle Peter was able to walk on water as long as his eyes stayed on Jesus, reason being because he had the living word of God right in front of him. But as soon as he turned away to life circumstances and off of the author of the wind and sea he started to sink. But in the midst of his trouble he cried out Lord save me. Jesus said he will never leave nor forsake us. When we waver away from being Christ-like, all we have to do is cry out, and the Lord will hear. As Christians when we look away from Jesus we lose that confidence in who we are. We tend to forget that we are Christ-like, because that natural man will soon show himself; he's not gone he just like Satan waiting to devour/ to take control all he needs is a thought to come forth that is not of God. 2Corinthians (10: 3-5) reads: (For though we walk in the flesh, we do not war after the flesh. For the weapons of our warfare are not carnal, but mighty through God to the pulling down of strong holds): Casting down imaginations, and every high thing that exalteth itself against the knowledge of God, and bringing into captivity every thought to the obedience of Christ.

We have to learn how to detach from our soul and follow after the spirit of God. We must get our soul to line up with our spirit, which causes us to have our mind transformed in to the mind of Christ. In being Christ-like, when we have put forth Gods word just stand; be unmovable always abiding in the work of the Lord. Don't let the devil or anyone else push us off of our post. We are to take root in the word of God. Jesus says to abide in him. John (15:1): I am the true vine, and my Father is the husbandman. John (15:4-7): Abide in me, and I in you. As the branch cannot bear fruit of itself; except it abide in the vine; no more can ye, except ye abide in me. I am the vine, ye are the branches: He that abideth in me, and I in him, the same bringeth forth much fruit: for without me ye can do nothing. If a man abide not in me he is cast forth as a branch, and is withered; and men gather them, and cast them into the fire, and they are burned. If ye abide in me, and my words abide in you, ye shall ask what ye will, and it shall be done unto you. What Jesus looks for in his people is

Christ-likeness. In order for us to be productive we must be discipline of the father just as he was. We must maintain an abiding union with the vine, when we abide in Christ. Our prayers are effective when we can walk as a Christian and not just talk a good game.

The more we feed on the word of God and allow the Holy Spirit to teach us, to guide us, to reveal all truth to us concerning Jesus; we will become more and more Christ-like. We cannot become Christ-like if we don't study to find out who Jesus is and what his purpose was and is; which is to do the will of God the father. To seek and save those who are lost, by spreading the gospel of Jesus, that is the mission of a Christian. We must remember nothing is impossible for a Christian when applying Gods word mixed with faith.

✍ *Keep our eyes on Jesus*

When Peter walked on the water faith told him he could. But he looked away from faith and allowed that natural man to invade his mind and tell him that this goes against science. He forgot that he was in the company of the creator of gravity, the one that could speak to the wind and the sea and they would obey. He did what we do forget our identity which is a spirit, the flesh will be with us until the day we die. So we need to know how to deal with it, and never forget that we are in charge of our body, our body is not in charge of us. The world is behind us the cross is before us. But every time we look behind us and set our mind on the things from our past, we resurrected that old man that we buried with Jesus. It's alright to give testimony to what or where the Lord has brought us from, but only if that wound is healed. If not, keep looking at the cross that is before you pressing toward the mark of the high calling of God. Philippians (3:13-14) reads: Brethren, I count not myself to have apprehended: but this one thing I do, forgetting those things which are behind, and reaching forth unto those things which are before. I press toward the mark for the prize of the high calling of God in Christ Jesus. Sometimes I can see the world as God had created it from the beginning and I look at what we have turn it into because of the lack of knowledge we have concerning ourselves. Hosea (3:6): My people are destroyed for a lack of knowledge, because thou hast rejected knowledge, I will also reject thee, that thou shalt be no priest to me, seeing thou hast forgotten the law of thy God, I will also forget thy children.

We are destroyed because we have forgotten who we are which is a spirit and have been chasing after the flesh which is of the dust of the ground. God breathed his spirit into us and gave us life, and not only that 1Peter (2:9) says: But ye are a chosen generation, a royal priesthood, an holy nation, a peculiar people; that ye should shew forth the praises of him who called you out of darkness into his marvelous light. Any time we turn back to the flesh, we forget who God says we are, that we have been redeemed, we are not in darkness anymore about who we are. We are Christians, Christ-like; our eyes have been open because of the light. That why we should know what being a Christian means which is having the mind of Christ. We can do what Jesus said we could do he would not have told us if it couldn't be done. God always gives us the grace to complete what he has called us to do. Just as Jesus told his disciples I prayed for you that you might not fall into temptation, he is also praying for us at the right hand of the father. There is no greater prayer than the prayers of Jesus for us. So don't be fearful Jesus is in the midst of whatever we do. God also says in chapter (3) of Hosea: That we forgot the law, he gave us a commandment to love one another as he has loved us, and put no one before him. He said that he will forget our children, why? Because we have forgotten his only begotten son Jesus and we have put everything ahead of Jesus. We continue to forget that we are a Christian, and the one that we represent is Christ Jesus our Lord and Savior.

Being a Christian is not just something we do for show, it's who we are we have been washed in the precious blood of Jesus and adopted in the family of God; so therefore walk accordingly as he has walked. Jude(1:20-25): But ye, beloved, building up yourselves on your most holy faith, praying in the Holy Ghost, keep yourselves in the love of God, looking for the mercy of our Lord Jesus Christ unto eternal life. And of some have compassion, making a difference: And others save with fear, pulling them out of the fire; hating even the garment spotted by the flesh. Now unto him that is able to keep you from falling, and to present you faultless before the presence of his glory with exceeding joy: To the only wise God our Savior, be glory and majesty, dominion and power, both now and ever. Amen.

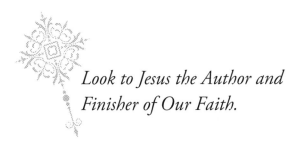

Look to Jesus the Author and Finisher of Our Faith.

Why do we trust so much in the things of man and in our riches, instead of the things of God? Hebrews (12:2) clearly says: Looking unto Jesus the Author and Finisher of our faith. That means that Jesus is the beginning, all that is in between and the ending of our lives. He is the first and the last, and not just our lives but of everything that was ever created seen and unseen. Genesis (1:1-2): In the beginning God created the heaven and the earth. And the earth was without form and void; and darkness was upon the face of the deep. And the Spirit if God moved upon the face of the waters. And the chapter goes on to say that God continued to create in the earth and the last thing he did was to form man out of the earth. Then he put man to sleep and created woman from the man's rib. On the sixth day God ended all his work which he had made and God rested on the seventh day. The Lord has already written our lives out, something that man cannot do. Man cannot tell us what tomorrow holds for our lives or even if we will see tomorrow. That's why we need to be looking to the author and finisher of our life, which is Jesus. Everything that man has made, and the knowledge that he has was placed in him by God our heavenly father.

Why does it seem easier for us to believe that the world just evolved; rather than to believe that there's someone so powerful that he could create the whole universe? I think we all know deep down inside of us that this world didn't just appear all by itself. But because we say we cannot see God physical, it seems more believable to some of us to think that man did it all. If you can tell me how a man that is on the same level as we are (meaning born of a fleshly body), that can be killed as quickly as you or I can; how could he create this world? I can tell you how I have seen God and still see him until this very day. I feel him when I lie down at night and can sleep in peace, because he said that he has giving his angels charge over me to protect me. Not only when I am asleep but everywhere I go, I feel his presence every morning when he gives me a gentle touch of his love to wake me up. I feel him when I take a breath, when I open my eyes, when I place my feet on the floor and can stand. He gave me my health and strength, when I walk outside I see God everywhere I look. I see what God has given man the ability to do. What we don't realize is that everything that happen in this physical realm must first manifest in the spiritual realm; but in saying that God is not the author of evil or confusion. The author of our lives came so that we would have life and have it more abundantly.

The evil in this world is that of the devil which comes to kill, steal, and to destroy, and he uses man who is still in darkness; because he refuse to believe in the author and finisher of life. Man wants to believe in himself and he is still blinded by Satan and his devices thinking that he is in charge and he's not. Satan has managed to deceive man into believing that there is no God, no heaven, or hell. And that we all just appear and when we die we'll just go back to where we came from. Question if we don't believe in the Lord where did we come from and where will we go when our time on this earth ends, sense man has all the answer? The Bible says that everything was created for the Lord, by the Lord and without him was nothing created that was made.

2Kinsg chapter 6 opens our eyes to the fact that there is a world that exist that we cannot see with our physical eyes, but we have an amazing heavenly father that can open our eyes and our heart to see the unknown. But then why should God have to prove himself when he has already giving us his all and his best, the Lord Jesus Christ. Jesus said blessed are those that believe without seeing. 2kings (6:14-17): Therefore sent he thither horses, and chariots, and great host: and they came by night, and compassed the city about. (15): And when the servant of the man of God was risen early, and gone forth, behold, an host compassed the city both with horses and chariots. And his servant said unto him, alas, my master! How shall we do? (16): And he answered, Fear not: for they that be with us are more than they that be with them. (17): And Elisha prayed, and said, Lord, I pray thee, open his eyes, that he may see. And the Lord opened the eyes of the young man; and he saw: and, behold, the mountain was full of horses and chariots of fire round about Elisha. To believe the impossible we must first see the invisible, Elisha did not ask God simply to show his servant another miracle; he asked for his servant to see into another dimension. The Lord opened his eyes and he saw that the mountains were full of horses and chariots of fire all around them. With men things are impossible, but with God nothing is impossible. So why do we put so much trust in man than in Jesus who is the author and finisher of our faith.

We cannot build faith to do supernatural things by looking to man, but we can build our faith to do supernatural things with our Lord and savior Jesus Christ. The Bible says in Philippians (4:13) I can do all things through Christ who strengthens me. The Lord knows our beginning and our end; he has all the power in heaven and in the earth. Man didn't die on the cross for us, neither did man go to hell and preach to those that were in captivity and set them free, that was nobody but Jesus. Jesus said that he would never leave us nor forsake us. Even if we can't see him with our natural eyes, we have the faith to trust him at his word. The Lord said that his word will not return void, it will do just what he said it will do. We must realize that Jesus is the only man that has ever died went to hell and was resurrected; the Bible says that he is the first born from the dead. The Lord is the only one that can bless us, the only one that can love us unconditionally no matter how many times we have disappointed him. While, man tend to turn his back on us the Lord will protect us from seen and unseen dangers. Man is running around destroying one another mentally and physically. We can go to the Lord and tell him all our secrets and not have to worry about anyone finding them out, or him judging us. The Lord has forgiven all of our sins while man continues to hold them over our head. The Lord teaches us to love our enemies, while man can't find it in himself to love his enemies. The Lord say to pray for those who despiteful use us, but man say I will stop giving to those who try and use me, not realizing that God is setting us up to be blessed by him.

Number (23:19): God is not a man that he should lie; neither the son of man that he should repent: hath he said, and shall he not do it? Or hath he spoken, and shall he not make it good? It is impossible for God to lie because whatever he speaks out of his mouth will manifest, unlike man we can't not even control our tongue. James (3:3-8): Behold, we put bits in horses' mouths that they may obey us, and turn their whole body. (4): Behold also the ships, which though they be so great, and are driven by fierce winds, yet are they turned about with a very small helm, whithersoever the governor listeth. (5): Even so the tongue is a little member and boasteth great things. Behold how great a matter a little fire kindleth!

(6): And the tongue is a fire, a world of iniquity. So is the tongue is so set among our members, that it defileth the whole body, and setteth on fire the course of nature; and it is set on fire of hell. (7): For every kind of beasts and birds, of serpents, and of things in the sea, is tamed, and hath been tamed by mankind: (8): But the tongue can no man tame; it is an unruly evil, full of deadly poison. Man can't even control what he speaks without the aid of the Holy Spirit, but yet we seem to have more trust in man than in the Lord. God can't go back on his promises because he is all powerful, man can break a promise without notice. God speaks of love towards us; man when he speaks if he is not governed by the leadership of Jesus will tend to speak more evil about someone then good. Are about how we can manipulate, or get over in life, it becomes all about me, myself and I. Romans (7: 18-21): For I know that in me (that is in my flesh,) dwelleth no good thing: for two will is present with me; but how to perform that which is good I find not. (19): For the good that I would I do not: but the evil which I would not, that I do. (20): Now if I do that I would not, it is no more I that do it, but sin that dwelleth in me. (21): I find then a law, that, when I would do good, evil is present with me. Throughout this life a conflict goes on between the new nature and the old. That's exactly why we must look to the author and finisher of our lives, because he has done what no man has ever done given us a way out of ourselves, he has given us a way to victory.

Christ frees us to live in the power of the Holy Spirit. Man has limitations Jesus doesn't, what happens if we keep turning to man and never accept Jesus; because we thought man was the solution? Than we take our last breath believing more in man, (make this question personal); where do you think you will spend eternity? Man can't help us then because they are just as we are human, Gods creation. Jesus can't help us either because it will be too late we will have lost our right to make a conscious decision. God is a supreme being, He is the most high, the all mighty, the first and the last, the everlasting. He is the Holy One, Omnipotence (all powerful), Omnipresence (Ever-present), Omniscience (All-knowing), He's of great mercy, forgiving, wise, patient, loving and kind, slow to wrath (angry). I could go on and on about who God is, there is no comparison between God and man. We are made out of his image not out of ourselves. Looking to Jesus the Author, and Finisher of our faith, God bless.

Obedience is The True Proof of Faith.

Obedience is defined as being submissive to the restraint or command of authority. Proof is the evidence that compels acceptance by mind of a truth of fact or the operation that establishes validity or truth. We have validation in the word of God from the beginning of creation, John (1: 1-5): In the beginning was the word, and the Word was with God, and the Word was God. (2) The same was in the beginning with God. (3): All things were made by him; and without him was not anything made that was made. (4): In him was life; and the life was the light of men. (5) And the light shineth in darkness; and the darkness comprehended it not. In the beginning links Jesus the word with the God of creation. The word is Jesus Christ, the eternal, ultimate expression of God. In the book of Genesis God spoke the world into existence; in the gospel God spoke His final word through the living Word, His Son. The phrase 'the Word was God' attributes deity to the Word without defining all of the Godhead as the Word. John (1:3) declares that Jesus was the divine agent who was responsible for the entire creation. If we really trust and believe in the word of God, we will be willing to do any and everything that his word clearly states that we can do through Jesus our Lord and Savior. Testimony is evidence based on observation or knowledge, a solemn declaration made by witness under oath; confirmation, proof, testament. We have the witness of God the father concerning who Jesus is. John (8:17-18):

It is also written in your law, that the testimony of two men is true. (18): I am one that bear witness of myself, and the father that sent me beareth witness of me. In God we have witness of whom Jesus is, and that is the word of God made flesh.

Number (23:19): God is not a man that he should lie; neither the son of man that he should repent: hath he said, and shall he not do it? Or hath he spoken, and shall he not make it good? Whatever God says about Jesus is true and what he says we can do through his word in the name of Jesus is true. It's up to us to believe it and the proof that we believe it is by our faith; and walking in obedience will prove our faith. Isaiah (55:10-11): For as the rain cometh down and the snow from heaven and returneth not thither, but watereth the earth, and maketh it bring forth and bud, that it may give seed to the sower, and bread to the eater. (11): So shall my word be that goeth forth out of my mouth: it shall not return unto me void, but it shall accomplish that which I please, and it shall prosper in the thing where so I sent it. Let us look at the life in which we are living today; are we obedient or disobedient to the will of God? If we are in his will then we would not have a problem with obeying his word. Romans (10:17) tells us that faith comes by hearing and hearing by the word of God. Our obedience to God's word shows proof that we believe and trust in him, this is our step of establishing our faith. Now that we are establishing faith in God, he is just and true to carrying out the promises that he has made to us concerning those of us that are obedient to his will.

If we are not acting on the will of God there is a penalty for disobedience, but there is also a reward for being obedient. When you are in disobedience you are being rebellious against the authority of God. Now, let's look at the penalty of disobedience that man has experience throughout his life. Paraphrased: The book of Exodus tells us that God used his servant Moses to bring his people out of bondage in the land of Egypt. Exodus (3:7-10): And the Lord said, I have surely seen the affliction of my people which are in Egypt, and have heard their cry by reason of taskmasters; for I know their sorrows; And I am come down to deliver them out of the hand of the Egyptians, and bring them up out of that land unto a good land flowing with milk and honey; Now therefore behold, the city of Israel is come unto me: and I have also seen the oppression wherewith the Egyptians oppress them. Come now therefore, and I will send thee unto Pharaoh, that thou mayest bring forth my people the children of Israel out of Egypt. God sent his servant Moses to be his massager to Pharaoh to let his people go. Moses asked God whom shall I say sent me and God said to unto Moses I AM THAT I AM: Pharaoh would not hearken to Gods command, so God harden Pharaoh's heart, and multiplied with signs and great wonders in the land of Egypt: God harden Pharaoh heart, because he want them to know that it was not because of Pharaoh might that the people of Israel was freed but because of God. The people of Israel were freed but through the process of their journey God made provision for their every need, but they murmur and complaint and ultimately the people turn their back on God and made them an idol God and because of their disobedience. The book of Numbers chapter (14) tells us that they could not enter in the promise land, the people has to wonder in the wilderness forty years because of their unbelief. Numbers (14:34-35): After the number of the days in which ye searched the land, even forty days, each day for a year, shall ye bear your iniquities even forty years, and ye shall know my breach of promise. (35) I the Lord have said, I will surely do it unto all this evil congregation that are gathered together against me: in this wilderness they shall be consumed, and there they shall die. If we truly have faith in the word of God then we will be obedient to what the word says we will use it in the principle and governing of our lives. We would not doubt God's word concerning who we are, what we can do, what we can have or where we can go.

When we are obedient to God's word it shows our faith, it shows that we trust in his word in all areas of our life. We cannot have true faith if we are not obedient to God's word. The Bible tells us that obedience is better to God than sacrifice. 1Samuel (15:22): And Samuel said, Hath the Lord as great delight in burnt offerings and sacrifices, as in obeying the voice of the Lord? Behold, to obey is better than sacrifice, and to hearken than the fat of rams. When we obey Gods word that mean that we submit to his authority and if we submit to his authority than we are in agreement with his word, ultimately showing that we are doing just as Matthews (6:33) we are seeking his kingdom and his will his righteousness first. So therefore we are putting his word first by obeying his word, and by doing so we are walking accordingly therein faith.

Anytime we are in obedience we are submitting to God authority and therefore we are walking in faith toward the grace which is given to us through Jesus our Lord and Savior. In order for us to walk in the power of God we must be obedient to walking in our faith. The Bible says that without faith it is important to please God. Hebrews (11:6): But without faith it is important to please him: for he that cometh to God must believe that he is, and that he is a rewarder of them that diligently seek him. Hebrews (10:38) states: Now the just shall live by faith: but if any man drawback, my soul shall have no pleasure in him. How can we walk in faith if we fail to obey God's word? In order for us to move in the word we must obey what the word says, because if we do not obey the word we will not put forth action. If we don't obey we are not submitting to that authority, therefore being in rebellion to the word. These are some people that were obedient to the word of God, or apply their faith in the word of God. Hebrews (11:5) Enoch's translation to heaven, without physical death, took place because he pleased God by taking Him at His word and living his life in obedience. Hebrews (11:7) shows Noah's obedience in building the ark far inland was physical evidence of his trust in God's word.

Hebrews (11: 8-10): Abraham demonstrated his faith by obedience in leaving his home in Ur and journeying to unknown lands, in living long years in the Promised Land as a foreigner in temporary quarters. Hebrews (11:11): Sarah gave birth to Isaac when she was 90 years of age because she looked away from her physical inability and judged God faithful to keep his word. We must lay aside anything that hinders our progress, when it come to being obedient to serving God. Obedience and Faith works hand in hand, because without obedience we will never move in our faith. Look at it this way if your parents told you that they were going to buy that car for you that you have been dreaming about and all you have to do too earn the car is to keep the house clean while they are out of town; when they get back and you have done nothing as far as cleaning, were you obedient to their word or disobedient? Did you do what they asked you to do in order for you to receive the car? Did you just sit back and believe that you would still get it by not moving on what they asked of you? That's how it is with our faith in God's word we must be obedient to walk in the word of God it shows that we trust His word when we are obedient to it.

Thinking on the Goodness of God

Do you ever really take time and think about how good God has been to you? You are the only one that can answer this question. Because no matter whom you have told or what you have told them about what God has done for you, you still have only touched the surface of what God have really done. You haven't really taken the time to sit and meditate on everything that God has done for you. Because most of our lives we had this delusion that everything that has happen in our lives was by our own self effects. You are the only one that knows what God have brought you through and not only that, but how he has open doors for you that no man can close. Revelation (3:7) states: And to the angel of the church in Philadelphia write: These things saith he that is holy, he that is and no man openeth. In your quite time when no one else is around and you have settled down from all of the business throughout the day, when you have closed the world outside your door, do you ever just stop and think about how good God really had been to you? That if it had not been for the Lord you would not have made it thus far; some time we tend to forget in our busy live that God is the answer to all of our need: mentally, physical, spiritually, emotionally, and financially. God has allowed us to cast all our cares upon him; 1Peter (5:7) reads: Casting all your cares upon him; for he careth for you. If we give God all our anxieties we know with confidence that He will handle everything for us because he loves us.

The Bible says that even when temptation comes God has already provided a way for us to escape all we have to do is to trust him. We have a loving father that has already made a way out of no way. God has blessed us to be the head and not the tail, to be above and not to be beneath, to be the lender and not to be the borrower. God has giving his only begotten son who has died in our place. And he didn't stop there he went to Hell so we wouldn't have to; rose from the grave with all power in his hand. Jesus did it all just for you and me. Just to think of the goodness of the Lord should make us fall deeper in love with him. There is no one that will ever love us the way Jesus loves us are take care of us the way he has committed to do. We have messed up so many times and still when we mess up he stands with loving arms saying to us in Matthew (11:28-30): Come unto me, all ye that labor and are heavy laden, and I will give you rest. Take my yoke upon you, and learn of me; for I am meek and lowly in heart: and ye shall find rest unto your souls. For my yoke is easy, and my burden is light: Jesus offers us an open, free, and loyal relationship with him. Jesus doesn't want us all burdened down or stressed out, he doesn't want us to wait until we get to heaven to have a great life. Jesus wants us to have heaven on earth in him and through him.

How many times can you look back over your life and realize that there were a lot of situations that you now know that you should not have made it through? How many times has it been that you had no clue where your next meal was going to come from and suddenly you have more than enough, or those bill that got paid, or someone blessed you and paid your rent or house payment. In case you didn't know it was all orchestrated by the hand of God; God knows what we have need of before we do. Philippians (4:19): But my God shall supply all your need according to his riches in glory by Christ Jesus: It's not according to our riches but according to his; our father owns everything, he created all.

✎ *God has worked it all out*

God has given us eyes to see, even if you have lost your physical sight or was born into this world without physical sight trust and believe God doesn't make mistakes. We might not understand why but according to Romans (8:28) all things work together for the good to them that love the God and for those that are the called to his purpose. You don't have to have eyes to see because you have spiritual sight, and I believe that a person with spiritual sight see things that we can see. They see the beauty in people; the beauty of life that God has bless them to see internally where we tend to look first at the external. What a mighty and merciful God we server, He is longsuffering, slow to angry, gentle, loving, kind, faithful and true. God says that his grace is sufficient; meaning whatever, when ever, however, and where ever you have a need his grace has it covered. The goodness of God has delivered us from seen and unseen dangers God has given us unlimited favor. According to Mark (11: 23-24) tells us that we can have whatsoever we say if we shall not doubt in our heart, but to only believe what his word says we can have; we shall receive it. Jesus has done the hard part all we need to do is believe, but for most people it's hard to just believe that it could be that easy. We know we did nothing to deserve it or we find it hard to believe that God loves us that much; what we must remember God is not a man that he should or can lie.

God's goodness is not based on what we do or who we are it's based on who He is. It is God nature because he is love, his heart far surpasses our understanding no matter what we do he still loves us and want for us to love and except him. We may turn away from him but he says in his word if we will turn back to him he will in no wise cast us away. God's goodness has already done exceeding abundantly above all that we could ask or think according to the power that works in us; and we know if we have accepted Jesus we have someone greater in us than in the word. By the goodness of God we have the peace of Jesus; we can do all things through Jesus who gives us strengths according to

Philippians (4:13). The goodness of God can manifest perfection in us if we will just summit. Matthew (5:48): Be ye therefore perfect, even as your father which is in heaven is perfect, we have a heavenly father that is perfect and if we allow him too he will change us from glory to glory: We are to be imitators of him, nothing is impossible with God on our side. He has made us to be more than conquers through Christ Jesus. When I say be perfect it's more of a moral nature, but, on an all-inclusive love that seeks the good of all.

Instead of following the example of sinners who love only those that love them, we should strive to follow after God, in also loving those who don't love us. The Bible says that love never fails, that it covers a multitude of sin. When we think on the goodness of God if we were to be honest with ourselves we know that everything we are, and everything we have is because of God and nothing of ourselves. When we lay down at night and are blessed to wake up in the morning we know that it is because of the goodness of the Lord. God has giving us our health and strength, he keeps us clothed in our right mind. He made a way for us to have food and shelter, clothes to wear, a heart to love, made us a way to get around, and how many of us have taken the time to say Lord I thank you for all you have done.

✎ *God knows the purpose he has for us.*

God sees us through every heartache, every pain, he sees us through the good as well as the bad situations that happen in this life; God knows the thoughts and the plans that he has for our lives according to Jeremiah (29:11-14): For I know the thoughts that I think toward you, saith the Lord, thoughts of peace, and not of evil, to give you an excepted end. (12): Then shall ye call upon me, and ye shall go and pray unto me, and I will hearken unto you. (13): And ye shall seek me, and find me, when ye shall search for me with all your heart. (14): And I will be found of you, saith the Lord: The Lord is not hiding from us a lot of time we think that God is not with us, because we want our needs met at the very moment that we have prayed and ask him for something. Not considering what he has already done and the things he has given us which we never asked for; and God did that just out of his love that he has for us, and out of his goodness. That shouldn't always be the reason we go to God because we need something, it should be because we love him and because we want to thank he for what he has already done. Just to be in his presence is a blessing in its self.

The Lord says that we will find him when we search for him with all of our heart. Not that he is hiding he is always there but we don't notice because our heart is fixed on what we can get; rather than truly searching for him because of our love for him. When we take our eyes off physical things and search for spiritual things then we will find the Lord. What we give our attention to with all our heart is what we find, not when it's convenient and feels as if we need to make time. I am so glad that God is not a mere man, I'm thankful that he is an all loving Father. That has given his children chance after chance; I'm thankful that he said in his word that he will never leave nor forsake us. I'm thankful that he loves us even when we break his heart. I'm thankful that he sees in us what we don't see in ourselves. Through all of Gods goodness why is it so hard for us to do the smallest thing that he has asked of us; and that is to put him and his righteousness first.

Anyone in this world can give a testimony of something that God has done for them; even if they say they done believe in him it does not matter because weather you believe or not God is still whom he says he is and he has still done a work in your life.

And he is the writer and author of everything and every person in heaven, in the earth and underneath the earth, we may not all serve him but we are all his creation. In Gods goodness, even when we miss the mark he picks us up and encourages us to keep going. And not only that he gives us the strength also, he says if we seek him we shall find him, if we knock it shall be open to us, and if we ask it shall be given unto us. Psalms chapter (23): tells us that God has already laid out a plan to watch over us, allows us to rest in him and at the same time he provides for our every need; he keeps the water calm so we want fell in and drown, when we become weary are feel like we can't go on he will restores us back to good health. He has paved a path to righteousness for us to honor his name. We can be in the lowest time in our life feeling as if we are close to death and he keeps our mind in a state of peace and comfort. And we have no need to fear because he is forever with us, God has already prepare a table for us in the midst of our enemies, and he has anointed our head with his Holy Spirit and given us so much favor until we can't contain it all. And after all that he has given us angels name grace and mercy to follow and protect us all our lives until we make our journey home.

What's his Name?

The Prophecy of his suffering: He will be exalted, He will be disfigured by suffering, He will be widely rejected, He will bear our sins and sorrows, He will make a blood atonement, He will be our substitute, He will voluntarily accept our guilt and punishment, He will be buried in a rich man's tomb, He will justify many from their sin, He will die with transgressors. His name is Jesus the son of the living God the father of all creation in heaven and in the earth. Jesus is the man who died on the cross for your sins and mines. Isaiah (53:2-6) for he shall grow up before him as a tender plant, and as a root out of dry ground: he hath no form nor comeliness; and when we shall see him, there is no beauty that we should desire him. 3: He is despised and rejected of men; a man of sorrows, and acquainted with grief: and we hid as it were our faces from him; he was despised, and we esteemed him not. 4: Surely he hath borne our griefs, and carried our sorrows; yet we did esteem him stricken smitten of God, and afflicted. 5: But he was wounded for our transgressions, he was bruised for our iniquities: the chastisement of our peace was upon him; and with his stripes we were healed. 6: all we like sheep have gone astray; we have turned everyone to his own way; and the Lord hath laid on him the iniquity of us all.

If we know the man Jesus and all that he has done for us then we should have no problem surrendering our life to him, because he is the righteous. He has taken on Himself all sin and punishment for our wrong doing, so that we can be forgiven, healed, and made whole. Jesus is able to have compassion on us and make intercession for us because he himself experienced the pains and sorrows of life. He came to earth laid down his glory in heaven to come here as a fleshy man; to seek and to save the lost, to reconcile us back to God our heavenly father. To take back what Adam had given to Satan, our hope of eternal life; when we can't call on any other name, we can always call on Jesus. Through the name Jesus we have access to come before the throne of God. Through the name Jesus we can declare our healing, our joy, our peace through the name of Jesus we can declare our victory over the enemy.

What's his name, Jesus the precious lamb of God, Jesus that way out of no way, Jesus that lily in the valley, Jesus that very present help, Jesus that chief corner stone, Jesus that hope when all hope is gone, Jesus that bright and morning star. What's his name Jesus the Anointed one of God, Jesus the King of Kings and Lord of Lords, Jesus that wonderful counselor, Jesus the Holy one of God, there are so many name that will identify him, but all we need to know is that when we call on him he will be there. Does not matter when we call, we can call him in the morning call him in the evening call him late at night he will always answer because he said that he will never leave us nor forsake us why not give it a try. Jesus. Amen.

Knowing Your Enemy and The Seed He Plants.

The temptation of the world takes our attention away from the Lord, when the Lord clearly says in Philippians (4:19): But my God shall supply all your need according to his riches in glory by Christ Jesus. When we accepted Jesus as our Lord and Savor we became the children the light. Therefore we were transformed out of the darkness of our mind where we had no knowledge of our inheritance. Which are the blessing that or apart of being a believers, our eyes are no more covered by the darkness, but they have been open because of the life of the world which is Jesus. Being a Christians/ followers of Jesus means we have made the world our enemy. Now, when we were of the world we were not considered the world's enemy, because it's easy to be received when you are of the same mind. But the Lord tells his people to come from among them; be ye separated. The world is of the wicked one, the world feed off of hate for one another and imperfect love, but Jesus teaches love to all mankind no matter the age, the gender, or the race. Jesus says to love your enemies and to pray for those that use you. The world chooses to hate their enemies and to use whomever using them. People that have never been taught by Jesus on how to love or have not accepted the love of Jesus don't really know what true love is. Love took Jesus to the cross carrying all of our sins, and kept him nailed there until everything was finished.

We learn how to love from imperfect people just as we were; we had flaws without Jesus. They could only teach what they knew love to be, but the love of Jesus is far above our comprehension. His love is unconditional; he loves us without reason, he loves us just because.

We didn't have to do anything to win his love, his mercy or his grace. It was a gift and when someone gives a gift all we have to do is accept it; because you can never do anything to earn a gift, if it has to be earned it's not a free gift. Ephesians (5:1-2): Be ye therefore followers of God as dear children. And walk in love, as Christ also hath loved us, and hath given himself for us an offering and a sacrifice to God for a sweetsmelling savor. Jesus gave himself as a sacrifice for us he didn't have to but he did it because of love. Not that we desired it but that's what unconditional love does, it thinks of everyone else before it thinks of self, love is selfless. Now because of whom we stand for we have made an enemy with the prince of this world, which is Satan, the devil, our adversary, that roaring lion. Ephesians (6: 10-12): Finally, my brethren, be strong in the Lord, and in the power of his might. Put on the whole armour of God that ye may be able to stand against the wiles (tricks) of the devil. For we wrestle not against flesh and blood, but against principalities, against powers, against the rulers of darkness of this world, against spiritual wickedness in high places. He says to be strong in the Lord and in the power of his might, because of our own selves we have no strength to fight against the devil. And even if we felt as if we could fight him, we can't fight what we cannot see this is a spiritual war far. We don't have the ability to fight against his tricks which comes in many different forms. The devil works in the realm of the mind, out thoughts our emotions he presents thoughts, ideas and subjections. 2Corthians (10: 3-5): For though we walk in the flesh, we do not war after the flesh: For the weapons of our warfare are not carnal, but mighty through God to the pulling down of strong holds; Casting down imaginations and every high thing that exalteth itself against the knowledge of God, and bringing into captivity every thought to the obedience of Christ.

Paul tells us to cast down those thoughts that have nothing to do with God or his word, to get rid of anything that tries to be above or come against the word of God. Satan tried to exalt himself to be like God when he was in heaven and got put out of heaven and now he wants to try and exalt himself into the mind of God's children; that's why we need to know our enemy. 1Peter (5:8): Be sober be vigilant because your adversary the devil, as a roaring lion, walketh about seeking whom he may devour. Satan is in a continually state of roaming to and fro looking to see if he can catch us with our armor off or even with a little crack in our hedge of protection. And that hedge or crack comes down when we get into doubt and unbelief in the word of God or when we are fearful. The Bible says that prefect love cast out fear. Satan feeds off of fear, God, works through our faith. The word of God says that my people perish from the lack of knowledge that's why we need to know Gods word so we know how to defend ourselves from our adversary/ enemy, we cannot speak what we don't know. John (10: 10): The thief cometh not, but for to steal, and to kill, and to destroy: I am come that they might have life, and that they might have it more abundantly. Satan our enemy comes to steal our joy, our peace, inflicted pain and heartache wherever he can he wants to keep us down in a state of depression, because if he can steal our joy our defenses come down. Therefore making us easy prey, he wants to take everything that we are and alternately take our life; So that he can try and take down the mission of Jesus. But what he fells to realize is that no matter what he does to come against us if we are walking with the Lord, and if we are standing on and being a doer of the word of God there's no way he can pull us out of the Lord's hands. We can only be pulled away if we allow him control if we take our mind off our solid foundation which is Jesus.

The Bible tells us in Hebrews (12:2): Looking to Jesus the Author and Finisher of our faith, but he only finishes what he starts. We must be careful whom we allow in our circle; because he will use the people that we love he has no problem using our parents, our children, anyone that can get close to us. Satan is the father of lies; there's no truth in him he is a deceiver. The Bible says that he comes as an angel of light, he will not fight against himself because in doing so his kingdom will not stand. So if we have someone in our life that is talking against the Lord know than, that is an enemy coming in the form of an angel of light. Be careful, we have to protect our anointing by surrounding ourselves with other believer's. The Bible says to forsake not the assembling of ourselves with other whom believers as we do; there is strength in unity. If you need to call on other believer's that fine; because the Bible say to strengthen your brother when he falls. But never forget that we have the high priest who name is Jesus and we can call on him at anytime day or night his ear is always open to our need, our prayers, and our desires.

He's seated at the right hand of God the father in heavenly places; interceding on our behalf, but he didn't leave us by ourselves he sent the Holy Spirit to help us in all that we do for the kingdom of God. The Holy Spirit is our comforter, our guide, our truth revealer, he bring things back to our remembrance. He is the power that is in us to be able to walk this walk of faith. He enables us in our calling that God has place in us, and if we learn to follow him he will walk us down that narrow path to Jesus that few find, because we tend to try and be the leader of him and not the follower. The Holy Spirit can warn us of scene and unseen danger. This battle can be as easy or as hard as we make it depending on our listening ability and what we believe in and stand for/ with.

Anything that happens must first manifest in the spiritual realm before we can see it in the natural. The word that we speak of God becomes a weapon a sword for the angels to fight our battle for us, but they cannot and will not go against our will. We just have to speak God word, have faith that it will do what he said it would do and then stand on it, it will not return void. The more we speak God's word in faith we give our angels a weapon to fight with on our behalf. Jesus took back the key, and he nailed everything to the cross. He went to hell took it off buried it and rose the third day with all power in heaven and in the earth. Now what we need to do is learn how to rest in the work that he has finished. And use the authority and the power of his name that he has given to us through his shed blood. All we have to do is call on that wonderful name of Jesus; the Bible says that demons tremble at the sound of his name.

They don't like the blood because Jesus blood is pure and full of light; demons can't stand to be exposed in the light. The things of darkness can't comprehend the things of the light. The Lord says to submit to him, and if we draw near to him he will draw near to us, and to resist the devil and he will flee from us. When we know whom we are fighting against and we know now that it is not the flesh; and we know his devices; it's already been won we just have to stand on what we know which is God word. Satan can't creep up on us if we keep on the whole armour of God. Ephesians (6:13-18)13: Wherefore take unto you the whole armour of God that ye may be able to withstand in the evil day, and having done all, to stand. 14: Stand therefore, having your loins girt about with truth, and having on the breastplate of righteousness; 15: And your feet shod with the preparation of the gospel of peace; 16: Above all taking the shield of faith, wherewith ye shall be able to quench all the fiery darts of the wicked. 17: And take the helmet of salvation and the sword of the spirit, which is the word of God: 18: Praying always with all prayer and supplication in the spirit, and watching thereunto with all perseverance and supplication for all saints.

We must at all times protect what we allow ourselves to be surrounded with what goes into our mind which are the thoughts that we allow ourselves to think. Our eyes which is what we are watching at all times, what we allow ourselves to listen to, or to speak out of our mouth all the areas must be guarded at all time, because if this areas are not protected it take root down in our heart where the issues of life are. The wrong thoughts will lead us off our mission, what we speak can either bless us or condemn us, what we listen to could determined our demise if we don't know who's voice to listen too. That's why we must keep walking in the word of God by faith continually, don't cease in our prayer life and always be thankful and continue in his will. Amen.

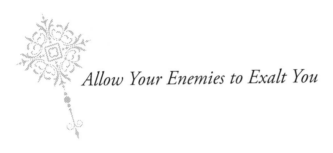

Allow Your Enemies to Exalt You

Jesus tells us that in this world we will have trials and tribulations but to be of good cheer because he has overcome the world. When we go through hardship in this life it is only to make us stronger, to move us to another level in our journey through this temporary life. The world is just preparing us for heaven. It is a way for us to be loosed from the old man which is corrupt and carnal minded, and be renewed in the spirit of meekness in the things of God. The world is our training camp and the devil and his host of demonic spirit or our testers. It's ok for us to catch hell, but don't let hell catch us, because when we catch hell we can control the amount of hell we will allow, and when we are tied of it we know who we need to call on when we want it to stop. But when hell catches us we have no control over what hell will put us through because we have allowed it to have the upper hand by not realizing that hell had catch us. What I mean when I speak of hell it is to be used as a metaphor speaking in terms of our trials and tribulations. Because that's what it feels like when we suffer the pains, the sorrows and all the hardships of this world not realizing that our trials and tribulations are to build us to stand strong in the Lord. It helps us to develop patience, knowledge, experience, and a hope into something that we can't see just yet, but believe by faith that it's all working together for our good.

We need to learn to use our enemies to exalt us higher in the Lord. For everything that the enemy comes against us with and we stand firm on the word of God it will take us to another level in Christ Jesus. When we are weak in an area of our live the devil knows this and he will continue to attack in that area until we learn to stand fast always abiding in the work of the Lord. We should always remember that as Christians if we suffer with the Lord we shall also rein with him. The Bible says that weeping may endure for a night but joy comes in the morning. So for every trial that we go through we should tell ourselves that it's morning times. Every time the devil tempt Jesus; Jesus response was it is written; he stood on the word of God no matter what came against him. He stood on the word and did not waver, that gave him victory over the enemy. He knew who he was and he would not be moved from the word or the will of his father. James (1: 2-4): My brethren, count it all joy when you fall into various trials 3: Knowing that the testing of your faith produces patience. 4: But let patience have its perfect work, that you may be perfect and complete, and lacking nothing. Being a Christian does not exclude us from difficulties it's more profitable for us because the situation from God's perspective viewing trials as a means of moral and spiritual growth, we do not rejoice in the trials themselves but in their possible results.

Our testing carries the idea of proving our genuineness. Trials serve as a discipline to purge faith of dross (waste) our sinful flesh. We need to look at trials and tribulation as a test, a way of cleaning us from the inside out. Every time a test comes against us we should stand fast in the word of the Lord knowing that it's already worked out for our good. We can't see it in the natural yet but it's taking place in the spirit. Look back when you were in school and you had to take a test but you realized that you did not study for that test the night before, you took the test and because you didn't study you failed that test. The good thing about it the teacher will give you a makeup test, now you are aware of the test and you have studied for it and because you are prepared now you passed that test. Now you can go to the next level or the next grade; that's how it can be with our journey in this life.

God has given us all the answers on how to handle every trial we face every tribulation that comes against us. And he gave us his Son Jesus as our example to show us that we can comes through the storms of life, the sorrows, and the pain. He has already defeated the fleshy body to show us that it can be done and then he gave his written word for us to study; so we would know how to take authority over all things in this life in Jesus name. We need to take what the enemy is trying to use to bring us down or destroy us and turn it around and use it to exalt us. To take us to another level in our walk with the Lord, in our walk to being just as Jesus is. The Bible says to let this mind be in you which is also in Christ Jesus. The more fire that comes against us the more we come out as pure gold if we stand firm. As a Christians we go through trials and tribulation we don't stay in them. If so than you are serving the wrong Lord; maybe you need to try Jesus, because he said that he will never leave you nor forsake you that he would be there until the end of the world. Let our enemies exalt us, every time he comes against us stand strong in God's word. When he sees that we will not be moved in an area that we once allowed him to defeat us in, but now have become strong he has to find another avenue to come down. Because that road is closed down for remodeling it's under new management. Every time we stand firm against him it build us up higher its help to tear down that old man, which is corrupt and to bring forth that new man which is renewed in the spirit of our mind; We will develop patience and temperance (self-control). We have to see the victory in every trial that comes against us, stop worrying about the problem and look to the solution which is Jesus Christ. Because he is that way out of no way, that hope when all hope is gone, that bright and morning star, he builds us up when we are torn down and he strengthen us where we are weak; he is our very present help.

Look to Jesus in all that we do, all that we go through, and be assured that it's already won. When Satan attacks us we need to use his tactics as a means of growth. Just as he used Adam and Eve to his advantage in the Garden of Eden, we must turn the table on him and use his own weapons that he comes against us with to exalt ourselves higher in the Lord. The Bible says Satan comes to kill, and to steal, and to destroy us, so why not use our haters to be our motivators. Proverbs (23:7): For as he thinketh in his heart, so is he: Eat and drink, saith he to thee; but his heart is not with thee, so if we think in our mind defeat then in our heart we are defeated also, but if we think in our mind that we are more than a conquer then so are we more than a conquers in our heart and then we want be defeated. Whatever we think we become: Mark chapter 11 tells us that we can have whatever we say if we believe and not doubt in our hearts. Jesus has already defeated our enemy and we don't have to battle him anymore, we just have to learn to rest in the finish work of Jesus. Jesus won the battle of flesh and has won the spiritual battle, now we must battle the spirit of our mind. Proverbs (24:16): For a just man falleth seven times, and riseth up again: but the wicked shall fall into mischief. see as believer's every time we get up we rise higher and higher, don't allow the enemy to keep you down, our strength comes from our test so let the test keep coming, let your enemy keep promoting you. Our enemy falls into mischief we fall and get up into growth. We must learn that when our enemy came against us we should rejoice because we are participating in a small part of what came against our savor Jesus Christ. It should be considered an honor if we look at it for what it really is; if it happened to a green tree why shouldn't it happen to a dry tree. So start using what the enemy comes against us with as a means to build strength in us and not something that we allow to tear us down. We are more than conquers in Christ Jesus. Don't stop your enemy from exalting you rest in the finish work of Jesus; and remember the joy of the Lord is our strength. We can do althings through Christ Jesus.

Don't Touch the Forbidden Tree

The first commandment that God gave to man was in the beginning of Creation; which was not to eat from the tree of the knowledge of good and evil, that commandment was given to Adam. The Garden of Eden was heaven on earth; it was paradise a place of perfectness, a place where God would come down to fellowship with man. God created man in his own image to take care of the Garden of Eden. Everything in the Garden was for man to enjoy; there were also two tree in the midst of the garden: Genesis (2:9): And out the ground made the Lord God to grow every tree that is pleasant to the sight, and good for food; the tree of life also in the midst of the garden, and the tree of knowledge of good and evil. Out of everything that God created there was only one condition one commandment for man, stay away from the tree of the knowledge of good and evil. God wills was to be done in earth as it is in heaven. After Adam and Eve's disobedience it caused God to banished them from the Garden of Eden; because if had they eaten from the tree of life we would have lived in a state of sin with no hope for the rest of our lives. We would have never seen death, but thanks be to God who loves us enough that he made away for us to have a second chance through Jesus Christ our Lord and Savior.

If we look at what the tree of knowledge of good and evil represents it was not only a tree that looked desirable for food, but it held all the good of life but also the evil that God wanted to shield us from. God's intent was for us to be like him, he never wanted our eyes to be open to sin/evil. Since time began we have been touching the forbidden tree; the things that God commands us to stay away from. The things that are not like him, thing that exalt themselves against him and his word; we can have the things in the world but we should let God be the one to give to us. Because what God give is everlasting and there are no consequences behind his giving. But when we get them through means of touching the forbidden tree which are the lust of the world it banishes us from the presents of God. When we pursue things instead of pursuing God first we are touching that forbidden tree. The forbidden tree looks good to the eye, but when we eat from or touch it; it opens our eyes to the works of the flesh which manifest: Adultery, fornication, uncleanness, lasciviousness, Idolatry, witchcraft, hatred, variance (dispute), emulations, wrath, strife, seditions, heresies, envyings, murders, drunkenness, revellings, and such like: This or the manifestations of touching or eating from the forbidden tree.

Jesus came so we could be restored from the actions of touching the forbidden tree, that through him we can eat from the tree of life everlasting. And the manifestations of the tree of life are find in him which are love, joy, peace, longsuffering, gentleness, goodness, faith, meekness, and temperance; if we abide in Jesus this hope, this victory of eating from the tree of life will be ours. Galatians (6:7): Be not deceived; God is not mocked: whatsoever a man soweth, that shall he also reap. If we continue to touch that which is unclean it will manifest eternal damnation. We have a choice to turn away from the forbidden tree and turn to the tree of life which is Jesus our Lord and Savior. There is sickness on the forbidden tree, but the tree of life offers healing: Isaiah (53:5): But he was wounded for our transgressions, he was bruised for our iniquities: the chastisement of our peace was upon him; and with his stripes we were healed. There is everlasting sorrow on the forbidden tree, but there's peace on the tree of life:

John (14:27): Peace I leave with you, my peace I give unto you: not as the world giveth, give I unto you. Let not your heart be troubled, neither let it be afraid. There is lack on the forbidden tree, but there is abundance on the tree of life: Now unto him that is able to do exceeding abundantly above all that we ask or think, according to the power that worketh in us, and according to 1Jonh (4:4): We have the greatest power in us than his that is in this world and that is the power of the Holy Spirit of God. Through touching or eating from the forbidden tree we are in bondage, but through eating from the tree of life we have been set free: John (8:36): If the Son therefore shall make you free, ye shall be free indeed. Galatians (5:1): Stand fast therefore in the liberty wherewith Christ hath made us free, and be not entangled again with the yoke of bondage. If Jesus has made us free why would we want to go back and play around with the forbidden tree which had us in bondage? Why not walk in the freedom that Christ purchased for us? Stop submitting to a religious or moral code, religion can look good hanging on the forbidden tree, but if the inside is not changed then it has deceived us as it did the Pharisees. Jesus told the Pharisees that they look good on the outside but their inside is full of dead man bones. Be careful there is deception on the forbidden tree that will lead us down the gateway to damnation:

Matthew (23:24-28): Ye blind guides, which strain at a gnat, and swallow a camel. 25: Woe unto you, scribes and Pharisees, hypocrites! For ye make clean the outside of the cup and of the platter, but within they are full of extortion and excess. 26: Thou blind Pharisees cleanse first that which is within the cup and platter that the outside of them may be clean also. 27: Woe unto you, scribes and Pharisees, hypocrites! For ye are like unto whited sepulchers, which indeed appear beautiful outward, but within full of dead men's bones, and of all uncleanness. 28: Even so ye also outwardly appear righteous unto men, but within ye are full of hypocrisy and iniquity. Jesus was illustrating their spiritual blindness, which allowed them to see trivial matters while over looking gigantic items; they paid detailed attention to matters pertaining to ceremonial cleansing, while ignoring God's demands for inner holiness, outwardly they appeared to be righteous, but inwardly they were morally defiled. The forbidden tree will beguiled us if we eat from or touch it, it will not only deceive us it has the means to seduce us. It takes the form of whatever our desires are, whatever we think that's what it will be; that's why we must have a heart transplant and a renewed mind by turning to the tree of life; this tree will never deceive us or seduce us to do wrong.

If we eat from the tree of life it will cleanse us from the inside out, it will constrain us to live righteous, holy, and true. We have been touching and eating from that forbidden tree since the beginning of creation and all we have reaped is never ending destruction, hardship, life pains, sorrows, hatred, betrayal by love ones, trouble on every hand, but yet we keep pulling from that forbidden tree thinking that it will be a change in our condition. There will be no change until we change the desire of the tree we choose to pluck from. It's all about the choice we make that will change our circumstance, and our eternal life. The forbidden tree to the fleshly body is like a magnet it draws and allures the flesh. The flesh desires everything that is not good for it, the Bible says that the flesh knows no the things, and therefore cannot please God because it cannot understand the things of the Lord. The flesh craves the wickedness of the world, the things that are contrary to seeking God and his righteousness first. The forbidden tree will always desire to be put first, if we continue to touch or to eat from it.

It will have us thinking that life is just about us, just about having fun, about working our life away, and not looking to God who is our source. Not giving God any me time, not giving him the reverence that's due to him. That same tree got Adam and Eve put out the heaven on earth that God had created for us to enjoy and to fellowship with him. We still cannot seem to walk away from what drives us to destruction and death. The forbidden tree knows how to speak to our mind; it knows how to persuade us if we are not connected to the tree of life. These two tree stood together in the Garden of Eden, and for those that have not turned away they are still standing together which one will you be drawn to the forbidden tree or the tree of life. The forbidden tree will always cause you to get farther and farther away for the tree of life. It will continue to take our life on a rollercoaster ride that will never end and the result is everlasting damnation. But the tree of life will freely care for and nurture us and through Jesus we have access to eternal life; and that tree will never change it will reminded the same yesterday, today, and forever.

So let us close our eyes to the forbidden tree and not touch or eat from it any longer, and open our heart to the tree of life. Don't allow the forbidden tree to drain the life from us. And don't allow it to continue deceiving us because it looks so beautiful to our eyes, sound so persuasive or seductive to our ears, feel so good when we touch it with our hands, and taste so sweet to our lips. Everything that looks good, feels good, sounds good and, taste good is not always good for us if it doesn't come by means of the tree of life. If we are going to sow let us sow to the spirit of the living God so that we can reap from the tree of life. Ask yourself a question has anything changed from the time Adam and Eve ate from the tree of the knowledge of good and evil? Has anything got better from touching or eating from the forbidden tree thus far? If you answered no then stop touching and eating from that tree, be sick and tired of going in a downhill journey. Stop being like the Israelites wandering in the desert for 40 years when it should have only taken 40 days. Jesus has given us away to the tree of life; let your choice be the tree of life for a better ending. The tree of the knowledge of good and evil was also created by God.

You say how could it be something that we should not touch or eat from considering it not all bad and it's not all good either? That was not the problem; the problem was that it was a commandment of the Lord and God has to be able to trust us with what he commands of us. He has to know that we will be obedient to his household, to his word. In looking at the way the world is there has always been an opposite too the thing in this life. Example—There's good and bad, there's hot and cold, wet and dry, faith and fear, love and hate, life and death, blessings and curses. But the thing to remember is that good can always stand alone on the other hand evil cannot stand, it would not exist without the presence of good.

Acknowledgement

First giving thanks to God who is the head of my life, who lead me by his holy spirit through the writing of this book, to my father and mother Alex and Rosa Lee Nored who are resting in the arms of Jesus, my children Jeffery, Lamar, and Courtney, along with my grandchildren, family and friends, and a special thanks to Roderick Brooks and Garry L. Thomas for all of their support. God bless you all.

Jesus is the way, the truth, and the life; when your trials and tribulations seem to wear you down turn to Jesus. When you feel all hope is gone turn to Jesus. When you need someone that will never leave nor forsake you turn to Jesus. Jesus is our very present help in all that we go through in this life.

This book will encourage all who are looking for strength, comfort, and spiritual guidance to turn to Jesus. A call to renew your commitment to the Lord and allow him to restore what is broken. If you have done all that you can do and still feel as if you are burdened down by life issues, this book will teach the readers how to let go and let God handle it all. Try Jesus his is the answer.

About The Author

Belinda is a native of Prichard, Alabama. She attends sure word Out Reach Ministry. She serves on the usher board and loves to video tape their Sunday morning service. This is one of the first of many books to come which was inspired by the Holy Spirit of God. I committed my life to the lord over 20 years ago. God has placed a gift inside of me and that gift is to share his message to the world. And that message is that no matter how bad things seem to be he is still on the throne. To God be the glory to God be the praise.